# *Creating Wealth Starts with Financial Health*

Discover and Overcome Behavioral Risks
in Your Financial Life

**Joel L. Franks**

**Creating Wealth Starts with Financial Health**
Discover and Overcome Behavioral Risks in Your Financial Life

Copyright ©2023 JOEL L. FRANKS. All rights reserved.
No part of this book may be reproduced in any form or by any mechanical means, including information storage and retrieval systems without permission in writing from the publisher or author, except by a reviewer who may quote passages in a review. All images, logos, quotes, and trademarks included in this book are subject to use according to trademark and copyright laws of the United States of America.

As a reminder, any views expressed are my own and are not the opinion of any entity unless otherwise mentioned in this book. And since we are critical-thinking creatures, these opinions are subject to change. For financial advice, consider consulting a licensed financial professional.

FRANKS, JOEL L., Author
CREATING WEALTH STARTS WITH FINANCIAL HEALTH
JOEL L. FRANKS

Published by
ELITE ONLINE PUBLISHING
63 East 11400 South
Suite #230
Sandy, UT 84070
EliteOnlinePublishing.com

ISBN: 978-1-956642-58-2 (eBook)
ISBN: 978-1-956642-56-8 (Paperback)

BUS069040
BUS027020

QUANTITY PURCHASES: Schools, companies, professional groups, clubs, and other organizations may qualify for special terms when ordering quantities of this title. For information, email info@eliteonlinepublishing.com.

All rights reserved by JOEL L. FRANKS and ELITE ONLINE PUBLISHING
This book is printed in the United States of America.

## Table of Contents

Introduction ................................................................. 7

Chapter One: Temper Tantrums ................................... 13

Chapter Two: Obsessions With Possessions.................. 27

Chapter Three: Riddle Me This...................................... 41

Chapter Four: Early Temptations................................... 53

Chapter Five: Needs And Nickels.................................. 65

Chapter Six: I've Been Framed....................................... 77

Chapter Seven: Navigationally Challenged ................... 91

Chapter Eight: I've Changed My Mind ....................... 109

Chapter Nine: Anchors Away....................................... 127

Chapter Ten: Your Reward Is Punishment .................. 139

Chapter Eleven: What If I Don't Like You .................. 151

Chapter Twelve: I Know What To Do......................... 161

Chapter Thirteen: What's The Special Occasion? ....... 173

Chapter Fourteen: I've Been Bullied By The Group ... 185

Chapter Fifteen: Life Is Short...But Don't Short-Change Your Lifestyle ............................................................. 201

Conclusion ................................................................. 215

# Foreword

As a "Money Energy Pioneer," helping others unleash their power and capacity to generate wealth through an enhanced relationship to money is my mantra. Creating opportunities to reach one's money energy potential greatly depends on understanding the impact of your emotions and behavioral variability on your financial decision-making. However, gaining a deeper psychological comprehension and appreciation is not as easily attainable. It takes someone with a passion for adult literacy and a keen ability to convey that knowledge in a friendly way that is digestible and retainable. And that's where Joel Franks comes into the picture.

I met Joel over 15 years ago at a conference where I was presenting solutions that allow us to tap into our behavioral-styles that could improve our relationship with money as well as help build and enhance advisor relations with clients. Both of which are intended to boost our financial decision-making outcomes. At the end of my lecture, Joel approached me and asked more probing questions in terms of the DNA Behavior discovery process and the benefits of helping others identify behavioral risks to raise awareness. Since then, we have maintained an ongoing business relationship for years—meeting up to explore the realm of behavioral economics and how best to utilize the learning lessons in actionable steps that lead to higher levels of money energy for the average person.

One of the biggest challenges of educating others on behavioral finance subject matter is how do you explain deeply emotional concepts and drive awareness, which can be grasped and converted into life changing action. When Joel informed me of his intentions to start his own firm and launch the FinWizdom podcast series, I thought to myself: Who better to accomplish this important endeavor than someone who is a talented storyteller and facilitator. His unique approach has always been a mix of educating and entertaining an audience in a way that leads to greater consciousness, and in turn greater financial well-being for those who are fortunate to listen.

Unfortunately, while podcasts are very popular, they are not for everyone and thereby have a limited reach. I think it was always Joel's intention to share his powerful stories through additional channels. When he informed me that he had embarked on this book, I was thrilled not just for him, but that he opened the doors to a larger audience with different learning styles who need to learn these invaluable lessons. If ever there was a book that could help people start their journey to improving their relationship with money, this is it.

*Hugh Massie*
Executive Chairman and Founder
DNA Behavior International

# Preface

A great deal of this book is derived from FinWizdom, a podcast series I created and currently host on this subject matter. It is my way of giving back. Leveraging my experience, expertise and empathy into learning lessons that can help others on their own road to financial well-being. But not everyone is an avid podcast listener and a great many followers have asked if these stories and more could be shared in a written format as a resource. It provides an opportunity to reach more people who have a strong desire to improve their own ability to manage money. The book itself is written intentionally as if we were engaged in a conversation versus a textbook style format.

So, if you're interested in understanding why you do what you do with your money, have a desire to learn how behavior impacts your ability to make sound financial decisions ... and you want to be entertained along the way ... I encourage you to continue reading.

Because creating wealth starts with financial health.

# Acknowledgment

I am grateful...

    For the life I have lived that feeds my passion and my purpose to help others

    For the loyal listeners of the FinWizdom podcast who value my words

    For the amazing friends who have been my pillars of strength and support

    For Evis (my wife) who is my biggest cheerleader, my inspiration, my love

# Introduction

Behavioral Economics—I have been in love with this field of study before I even learned there was a science behind our behavior and financial decision-making. Back then, I just called it "being smart with your money."

In the world of financial marketing and content development, which has been primarily my career path for over 25 years, the challenge has always been connecting with an audience in a way that strengthens customer relationships. Why? Because that's what drives purchases and loyalty to a given brand. And during that time, I have been fortunate to experience success and have been gainfully employed in several banking, insurance and investment firms.

Throughout my career, the financial products and intended audience may have varied, but my main objective has always been to help others improve their understanding of financial concepts, products, and services so that they could make informed decisions—preferably better. But what I've learned is that all our financial decisions are influenced by our emotions. No matter how informed you may think you may be or the knowledge-base you have aggregated, your choices are impacted by behavior. It was during my career, I pursued a deeper knowledge and certification in behavioral finance and chose to be an expert in applying those concepts to my work.

And you want to know what else I learned? I became a good storyteller. I realized I could lead others down a path to improving their relationship with money in a playful and practical way, which I found most adult financial literacy programs lacked. They often focus on feeding your brain the facts and concepts such as how money works, economics, basic budgeting, investment games, and so on. Those are all valuable lessons to be learned, but the most important story that needs to be shared is how your emotions shape your financial habits. Yes, your emotions do shape your financial habits.

Storytelling is one of the most effective ways to learn ... especially when it comes to behavioral economics (and you'll learn more about the topic in the first chapter). Telling tales is a powerful tool to help influence, learn, retain and inspire us to improve our relationship with money.

Think about how we learned math. Often we were given the problems to solve as just equations, but when it came to testing our comprehension, those problems were put into a story format. In its simplest context: Which was more useful to learning and recall: *"How much does 3 + 5 = ?"* .... or ... *"Jackie *has three apples and receives five more apples. How many apples does Jackie now have?"* See where I am going with this!

Storytelling facilitates narrative reflection, positive reframing concepts into snackable bites (for better retention), and thereby can be an incredibly useful tool to not only retain what you've learned, but it becomes a cognitive instrument in the decision-making process.

I think it's time to set the stage for YOUR story and for the chapters that follow with a question: Have you ever explored your relationship with money? I mean seriously explored your relationship with it?

The process of managing money is a balancing act between your wealth and income in relation to your financial needs, desires, and goals. And it's not just about setting a budget or a plan and then sitting back to enjoy the ride. It gets complicated. Market fluctuations, influential advice, peer pressure, social media, news briefs, life-changing events, unexpected expenses—all of which fluctuate as we pass through the various stages of our lives.

In fact, when it comes to managing money, you've probably heard at least one of these phrases in one form of media or another: Stay the course ... don't put all your eggs into one basket ... avoid buying high and selling low ... pay yourself first ... be wary of wants versus needs ... optimize your retirement programs ... build an emergency fund ... payoff high interest debt ... don't sit on too much savings, and the cliches go on and on.

Are you sick of hearing these and other similar quotes? Sometimes I am sick of hearing them too. So why do so many professional financial experts and the media keep using these expressions?

Well, first off...they're true! And while we consistently hear these lines of advice it's really hard to change your financial behavior. And even if you want to change, it's really hard to do. Have you ever tried to exercise more, stay on a diet, quit smoking or avoid the temptations of a sale? If you have tried any of these endeavors (or even attempted to stick to your New Year's resolutions), you know how hard this really is. Changing behavior is about our emotions.

This takes us back to building your financial literacy. There are many resources out there in the forms of informational websites, educational programs, community involvement, government initiatives—and that's all good stuff. You might have found them useful and have seen marginal improvement, but you might have also found it challenging to stick to the learning lessons. Often we fall back into the same habits we had before. Despite good intentions, many of these financial literacy channels can be viewed as a band-aid to the symptoms and not a longer lasting cure.

When it comes to financial wisdom, there is a plethora of self-improvement resources out there just waiting to be discovered. Much of the information you will watch or read often comes with rational recommendations and advice on how you can improve your financial decision-making. But there's just one catch. You're more likely to make choices based on irrational thinking and your emotions versus logic alone.

We often hear the question: "How can you take the emotions out of your financial-decision making?" I always wince whenever I hear that line because that's the wrong question to ask. It should be: **"How do you accommodate your behavior?"**

So how do you overcome behavioral risks? What are they? How can you tap into the learning lessons of behavioral economics? And for that matter, what is it?

Well, you're about to find out!

## Chapter One: Temper Tantrums
### Key behavior: Loss Aversion

*Have you ever witnessed a child begging to go on a ride at the amusement park that they were too young to enter, or a child denied the expectations of the purchase of a frozen treat when the sounds of the ice cream truck are heard in the distance, or maybe it's your own child, grandchild, niece or nephew making desperate pleas for you to buy them a new toy or asking you to download the latest app for their smartphone? And no matter what was said to justify the denial of access to that amusement park ride, the unbought ice cream, the unsuccessful procurement of a new toy or games for the phone...it only made the reaction worse...and that's when we experienced the temper tantrum.*

Temper tantrums are not a pretty scene. Just picturing that emotional outburst in a child and the potential for further escalation (regardless of the sound reasoning for saying "no") is cringeworthy. It's a good thing that we outgrow this phase of our lives as we become adults—or do we?

Have you ever shopped for apparel online or in a store and fallen in love with the way something might look on you or how well it complements your taste. What's even more enticing? It's on sale! But then comes the bad news: That clothing item, the one you just fell in love with, is out of stock in your size! When that happens, I'm guessing you are feeling frustrated and disappointed at that moment. However, was that the end of the story?

Did you just say to yourself "Oh well, that's that" or did you try and convince yourself that you could settle on a different style or size? Perhaps you even embarked on a journey to find the same garment elsewhere online or in another retail establishment, and the obsession grows to a point that whether or not it is on sale elsewhere—you want it.

This scenario is not limited to clothing either. This experience could easily have repeated itself if you recently discovered a new electronic gizmo, shopping for a car, replacing your kitchen cookware, or any number of items that have the potential to bring a sense of joy into your world—even if fleeting.

And this behavior isn't limited to tangible items. Are you someone who likes to play games on your smartphone? Have you ever been addicted to one that had multiple levels to complete and were stuck on a particular stage? In fact, every time you made an attempt to finish that stage, you felt you were that much closer and convinced yourself that you will make it to the next level THIS time. And speaking of time, how much time did you dedicate to this amusing distraction, while other, more pressing activities laid in waiting that may have been a bigger priority in your life?

This sense of frustration is experienced at work too. Have you ever been really excited to share your ideas, concepts or strategy to your co-workers or boss that you think rocks this world, that will drive revenue, efficiency or effectiveness for your organization. And yet when you shared this marvelous thought, I'm betting the response now and again was less than stellar. Even worse is when you receive little fanfare and the silent reaction is so deafening you could hear crickets. And if it wasn't the silent treatment, maybe you were given every possible logical reason why your great idea may not be so great. Did you say "ok, let's move on" or did you try to provide your compelling beliefs to double down on your idea?

Forgive the intrusion, but let's take this to a very personal level. Now I could be possibly wrong here, and this may be a wild guess, but maybe … just maybe … you may have experienced one or two disagreements with your friends, your lover or family member over the course of your relationship. Most often those disagreements are derived from situations where decisions need to be made about an activity, vacation, something for the home, or a problem you are facing. Maybe it's about my favorite topic: money. And if so, what lengths did you go to try to convince the other person that you are right and they are wrong.

In every scenario I just described (the obsession with the clothing purchase, the game playing, the work scenario or relationship squabble), you didn't handle rejection very well did you. And maybe you didn't visibly carry on like a child and start kicking and screaming in the middle of the room—although I have to admit the vision of an adult stomping their feet, screaming and running around the conference room at work is quite an entertaining thought. But you were, in your mind, throwing your own sort of temper tantrum. In your desire to exert control over your emotional response, you attempt to justify your feelings with facts that you are convinced defend your reasoning.

What I'm driving at is that we are imperfect beings and that these emotions we display or keep inside also impact our financial decision-making. And there is a field of study around this phenomenon. It's called **Behavioral Economics**.

Before we can define behavioral economics, we need to first define neoclassical economic theory, or in other words, traditional economics in terms of its fundamental assumptions. And forgive me, this is going sound a tad dry, but it's essential to understanding where BEHAVIORAL economics comes into the picture.

There are three assumptions to traditional economic theory:

#1 When it comes to decision making, people are assumed to know all possible outcomes and probabilities of a given situation.

#2 People are able to determine and measure the satisfaction that would be received from each of those outcomes.

#3 People have 100% of all the relevant information to make rational decisions about those outcomes.

These fundamental assumptions help in determining either the value of an asset or are used in making a particular decision given a number of constraints and resources. In terms of the study of economics, it's an underlying premise for economic models.

However, it is highly unlikely that you would ever know ALL possible outcomes, or ALL levels of satisfaction you would receive, or ALL relevant information in your financial decision-making hemisphere.

So how do we, as human beings, complete those gaps? We use what is called *heuristics*. These are the necessary shortcuts we use in our mind to help us make choices. They come in the form of our own experiences, the influences we gain from others, and the relevant facts and opinions we discover on our own. All of which equate to leveraging emotions.

And behavior and emotions, not logic, are the predominant determinants when individuals make financial decisions. Behavioral finance can be defined as: *a field of economics that explores how the actual decision-making process is influenced by social, cognitive, and emotional factors; and why and how behavior does not follow the predictions of economic models.*

In the introduction, I mentioned that taking the emotions out of your decision-making is not the right approach. It's how you accommodate your behavior. And how can we accommodate them? Well, there are dozens of behaviors and biases that go into your choices, selections, and convictions when formulating a feeling about what is best for you.

Consider those times you bought something on your credit card and it all made sense to you at the point of purchase, but when the monthly statement arrives in your inbox, you feel buyer's remorse and cannot help but wonder what were you thinking at the time?

Or maybe it's knowing how much you can afford going into the car dealership and yet leaving with an automobile that was beyond your budget, but convinced yourself you could afford it by taking from your emergency fund or taking out a slightly larger loan payment monthly.

This is especially true of investments where you felt confident performance was going to exponentially grow. Because I'm curious: Have you ever made an investment decision confident that the performance was sure to suck. WAIT-- WHAT?!! Of course that wasn't your intention going into the financial commitment. Who would? But you have limited resources in terms of information, time and advice to understand all the factors that would help with your decision to make that investment. Plus, you have all those unexpected risks in an industry, the market or influential global events. In all likelihood, your investment decision was impacted on what you have experienced, your emotional reactions to what you've read or watched, the opinions of those you deem as experts and your own personal belief system.

And this is where those adult temper tantrums come into the picture. Based on our limited scope of options and resources, we leverage our emotions and opinions to derive what we believe are the best choices. Simply growing up and becoming an adult doesn't automatically give you the ability and maturity to recognize and control those emotions, yet they play an important role in how we manage our money.

Let's dive into a little history about behavioral economics. Daniel Kahneman and Amos Tversky were two brilliant and curious minds who explored psychology starting in the late 1950s and early 60s. In the spring of 1969 these two met and explored cutting-edge experiments about how people learn from new information. Together, they published a series of groundbreaking and influential articles in the general field of judgment and decision-making, which culminated into the establishment of *Prospect Theory* in 1979.

Prospect Theory argues that those traditional economic assumptions mentioned earlier attempt to define rational behavior when people face uncertainty, but in reality fail to do so.

There's also a terrific line at the close of Dan Ariely's trailblazing book, *Predictably Irrational*.[1] That name may sound familiar if you are a follower of social sciences and psychology. He has published several other books, but I find that this one should have a place in your home library. Anyway, at the very end, Dan finishes his thoughts by saying "Economics make a lot more sense if it were based on how people actually behave, instead of how they should behave." I love the statement.

Most people don't know it as Prospect Theory, but you may have heard its other label: **Loss Aversion**. And there are three key principles at play here as well:

#1 People will exhibit more risk avoidance, or more risk seeking, depending on the nature of the outcomes that they can choose from.

---

[1] Ariely, Dan. Predictably Irrational, Revised and Expanded Edition: The Hidden Forces That Shape Our Decisions. Harper Perennial. April 2010.

#2 The value we assign to those outcomes depends on the perceived gains and losses relative to some form of reference point or prevailing assumptions.

#3 People generally avoid risks because losses loom larger than gains in our minds.

That last one is a really important statement.

You may or may not be familiar with the following illustration, but I sometimes like to ask this at parties or even with my Uber or Lyft driver when traveling more lengthy distances. So as an example, let's say you have $1,000 in your pocket, and I present you with two choices:

Choice A: I present you with a coin and with the flip of the coin heads I give you another $1,000 or tails you get nothing more in return.

Choice B: No coins to flip, I'll just hand over $500 to you.

So which will it be? Choice A, take a chance to double your money or gain nothing, or choice B: it's an automatic payday of $500.

Okay hold that thought because I am going to change the scenario. Now let's say you have $2,000 in your pocket, and once again I present you with two choices.

Choice A: I flip a coin, heads you pay me $1,000 or tails you do not need to pay me anything.

Choice B: Again, no coins to flip, but this time you simply pay me $500 and no chance of losing anything more.

Now which will it be, Choice A, the risk of losing $1,000 or nothing or Choice B, ust pay me $500 and call it a day.

When this study[2] was conducted by Kahneman and Tversky, an overwhelming majority of participants opted for Choice B in the first scenario and took the $500. The certainty of a gain of $500 outweighed the uncertainty of winning $1,000. Yet in scenario two, the overwhelming majority selected Choice A to flip a coin for the possibility of losing nothing versus paying $500. That's because we value gains and losses differently, despite, as in this case, the scenarios were statistically the same.

I have a personal example. Someone once gave me a wonderful bottle of wine, a relatively difficult to find red blend primarily made up of cabernet sauvignon, with a little Merlot and a touch of Syrah. I think it was valued at around $200. Of course, receiving such a gift made me happy. And a week later I went to open and enjoy this wine, when due to my clumsiness...I dropped the bottle! I can tell you that I was far more emotionally upset when that bottle shattered versus the happiness I was feeling in anticipation of drinking it.

---

[2] Kahneman, Daniel and Tversky, Amos. Prospect Theory: An Analysis of Decision under Risk. Econometrica. The Econometric Society. Vol. 47, No. 2 (Mar., 1979), pp. 263-292 (29 pages).

Loss aversion is a primary assumption of behavioral economics and many of the behavioral risks that are discussed within this book are subsets of it. Now you know the basics of how emotions impact your decisions, so now what?

Let's talk about ways to address emotions in your financial choices.

You can potentially reduce the impact of behavioral risks by feeding the brain with knowledge and awareness of the various heuristics and biases that you may experience, which can help improve your understanding of why you do what you do with money...it does not necessarily mean you will make the optimal choices with your money, but it may help you make the choice that is aligned with your behavioral tendencies and empower you with improved comprehension of the behavioral factors that you are experiencing in your own financial decision making process.

So what can you do now?

## Actionable Step 1:

*Finish reading the book!* Congratulations, you have already taken a step in the right direction by choosing to read this book. It's difficult to address the impact of your emotions without first becoming aware of the behavioral risks that influence your financial decisions.

**Actionable Step 2:**

*Breathe.* This is not an easy one, but it's similar to anyone who practices meditation or mindfulness. Whenever possible, take a moment before reacting and breathe. Take a look at your feelings as if you were a spectator. You may have heard this advice before, but here's the twist! Name the feelings or emotions you are witnessing. Are you able to see how they are influencing your decisions? If you saw these behaviors in someone else, what would be your observations?

**Actionable Step 3:**

*Use financial tools.* Thankfully in this modern age we live in, there is a plethora of useful financial tools and calculators online that are often free and can help you determine anything from how much house you can afford, calculate your risk tolerance level, useful budget programs to keep you focused, illustrations showing ways to pay off debt quicker, and detailed reports on most publicly traded investments, and, when it comes to investments...that leads us to number 4.

**Actionable Step 4:**

*Be wary of advice you read in social media, chat sessions, webinars, and reviews.* Sometimes it is hard to detect, but even advice and reviews can be influenced by behavior by those who present information. In addition, especially for investments, often you are reading about, and chasing after, yesterday's winners. It's why there isn't a single investment-related article out there that does not have that ever popular disclosure: *Past performance is not a guarantee of future results.*

**Actionable Step 5:**

*Consider behavioral risks.* When seeking professional advice, work with financial institutions and advisors who have incorporated behavioral risks as a consideration into their financial planning platforms.

These are just a few broad recommendations and we will continue to discuss more specific and actionable steps based on various types of behaviors in the chapters that follow.

So before you start screaming for some ice cream, take a time out and evaluate your motivations behind it.

# Chapter Two: Obsessions With Possessions

## Key behavior: Endowment Effect

*I'd like to take you back to your childhood for a moment. Do you remember when you were playing with your favorite ball in the yard and how much joy it brought you? But what happened when that ball went over the fence, or into the bushes, or some hard to reach place? I bet you were feeling anger, sadness, or even frustration. And what extremes did you go through just to get that ball again?*

Now that I have sent you to an early time in your life, I'd like to expand on this scenario ever so slightly. Let's say you and a few of your childhood friends were walking down the street and you came across a ball. It was just sitting there in someone's trash waiting to be hauled away for garbage. And as a group, you and your pals decide to take this new-found ball that was intended for trash, as an opportunity to go and play with it in a nearby open lot. And so, you and your buddies form a game using the ball. Everyone is having a blast until one of your friends kicks the ball over a relatively high fence that lies at the edge of the field, and into the trees that sit beyond a very wide stream.

At this point, it may take the next hour or two (and then some) to possibly gain possession of this ball. My question to you: Would you or any of your friends trouble yourselves over a ball that was destined for the garbage dump or does everyone just reflect on the good time just experiences and move on? Now unless there is a strong consensus to do so, I'm guessing that the odds are you and your friends seek out the next great adventure and leave that ball right where it is because it has no further value than the fun it offered at that moment.

Now, let's return to the original story and modify the scenario. What if it was your parents who bought that ball as a special gift just for you? It was given as a reward for completing your chores or some other good deed done. And like the previous story, you invite friends over to play with your brand new ball and everyone is having a great time. Until, once again, one of your friends accidentally kicks that ball over a similar fence, into a similar tree, across from a similar stream. I'm betting you WILL take an hour—or whatever it takes—to get that ball back! And why is that? Because that ball is YOUR ball. It was a gift, right? And that sense of ownership lends itself to a psychological influence called the **Endowment Effect**, in which we give an increased value to ideas and items that we attach greater ownership to. In other words, we have a stronger desire and emotion to hold onto things we possess.

And if you think this just happens in your childhood with your toys, here are a few examples where you might witness the same effect today:

It's like that seat in a classroom, or in a conference room, or even in your own family room where every time you return to that room there tends to be a particular chair that you gravitate to and you unofficially assign that seat as yours. In fact, this could even happen in a temporary situation such as the doctor's office. Ever been in a similar scenario where you sit in a chair and have gotten up to go to the bathroom and then when you return, someone is now sitting in the same spot you temporarily left? Tell me: How do you feel when you come back to find someone is sitting in "your" seat, and why should it even bother you? You don't own that seat in the doctor's office, or the one in that conference room, or the one in that classroom.

This not only occurs with tangible objects, but ideas too. I think the following has happened to everyone at least once who has ever worked for an organization where there is high interaction among several business partners. Think back to yesterday, a week ago or a month ago, when you had that ingenious idea that you were waiting to spring on your boss at the next one-on-one meeting. But, just a day before, during a conference call, someone else shares a similar idea that your boss and colleagues love and THAT person gets all the credit, not you. How does that make you feel? Are you feeling a little angry and mad at the person who had the same idea? You might feel it was stolen from you. Well why not, it was your idea, right? But yet you really don't own that idea until it is shared more visibly with others and anyone could come to the same conclusions and concepts as you did. This does not matter. You are upset because of the increased value to your OWN proposal versus a similar one derived from someone else.

Let me leave you with one other example relating to a fictitious tale. One I think many are familiar with. Remember the famous movies based on the books of J. R. R. Tolkien's *The Hobbit* and *Lord of the Rings*?[3] Remember Sméagol, who was corrupted by the Ring and transformed into that loathing creature named Gollum. Think about his story. He finds a magical ring; he did not forge it out of metal himself; he did not purchase it; he did not earn it (although he thinks he does); he is totally obsessed with possession. Gollum even calls the ring "My precious!" If that is not the endowment effect in its truest sense, I don't know what is. Talk about actions leading to destructive behavior and madness, when you empower objects you feel you own.

---

[3] Tolken, J.R.R. The Hobbit. George Allen & Unwin. September 1937; and The Lord of the Rings Trilogy. Between July 1954 and October 1955.

Okay, by now you may be asking yourself how does this impact my personal finances?

There is a commonly cited study conducted by some of my favorite behaviorists. In 1990 a study[4] was undertaken by Daniel Kahneman, Jack Knetsch & Richard Thaler where college students were willing participants in the hypothetical buying and selling of coffee mugs. They were nice mugs, but they did not have any unique characteristics either. Three groups were established. One group was given ordinary, ceramic mugs as "gifts" and then asked to sell them at a price ranging from $2.00 to $9.25. A separate group of students were asked to purchase those mugs to determine the price someone was willing to pay for one (using the same price range) and the last group was given the choice of mug or money (again within the same price range).

So here is the interesting outcome of this experiment. Those who were not in possession of a mug were willing to pay an average of $3.00. But those who received their mug that was gifted to them, valued them at a higher price, in fact, a much higher price. On average they were willing to depart with their precious mug for an average price of $7.00. The point is that once a sense of ownership of the mugs was established by the participants, the compensation they sought for the mug was

---

[4] Anomalies: The Endowment Effect, Loss Aversion, and Status Quo Bias. Journal of Economic Perspectives VOL. 5, NO. 1, Winter 1991 (pp. 193-206).

approximately twice as high as the amount others were willing to pay to acquire the same exact object. You would think it was irrational to not sell something that was given to you for free, but that is the power of the endowment effect. That is why, going back to our story about our childhood, you are going to spend the rest of your day obtaining possession of that ball regardless of obstacles.

As a side note, another study[5] conducted in 2000 by Ziv Carmon and Dan Ariely found that participants in an experiment involving the trading of hypothetical NCAA final four tickets sold at a price 14 times higher when participants "owned" the tickets for sale in comparison for the price others were willing to pay.

Maybe this sounds a little strange to you, or perhaps you are telling yourself that you could overcome these influences. I'd like the opportunity to reflect on a few situations in your own life that may get short-circuited by the same behavioral risk, when it comes to financial decision-making.

Let's start with a money back guarantee or free trial offer of a product or service. First off, these terms make you feel less adverse to a purchase as the risk of making a poor decision is minimized. However, once you have acquired that product or

---

[5] Focusing on the Forgone: How Value Can Appear So Different to Buyers and Sellers. Journal of Consumer Research, Volume 27, Issue 3, December 2000 (pp. 360–370).

service, you build a sense of ownership and value to it. This makes it tough to return the item because the longer you have it in your possession, the less likely you are to return it—even if you have a level of dissatisfaction.

Or how about this one: Have you ever been in the market for a new car? Maybe you had a specific model and color in mind. Let's say, as an example, you were thinking of purchasing this year's model in red and without all the bells and whistles to reduce the cost and yet satisfy your needs. So, you head over to the car dealership, but the particular model you seek is not in stock. No problem. They can order the vehicle you are asking for, but one of the reasons you went to the showroom is to take a test drive. The salesperson gives you the keys of a similar model that is sitting in the lot today so you can get a feel for how the car handles. It's not the color you were seeking; it's blue. It also has many add-ons such as the latest digital technology, the deluxe all-passenger sunroof, heated seats, upscale stereo system, etc. None of the perks you were seeking to obtain in the model you planned to order. That's fine because this is just a test drive.

So, you hop in, take it for a spin, get comfortable, it drives well and before you know it, positive inferences are kicking in. You start taking emotional possession of it and the dealer is counting on the endowment effect to increase the probability that you buy that car today to close the deal, instead of ordering the one you have to wait to receive several weeks from now. In fact, how do you feel after you complete the test drive and start walking back into the dealership lobby, when in the corner of your eye you spot another potential buyer looking over the same car in the lot? Kind of like the possession of the seat in the conference room mentioned earlier, right?

And if you think sitting at home all day reduces your chances of this behavior risk, think again. Consider today's technology. Let's say you are shopping for a new TV or new clothes to wear and the seller has an Augmented Reality option (or AR option for short). This technology allows you to see what that TV will look like right in your living room, or how that outfit will look on you without stepping into a fitting room to try it on. (This also falls into another concept called *nudging*, but we'll save that topic for another chapter.)

And what about stocks you may own. If you maintain your own investment portfolio, I am guessing you might have what is called a "media darling" or two that are heavily weighted in your stock lineup. Those are stocks which may have received frequent and very favorable attention in the news media at one point or another. They were, at the time and still may be, ideal investments. But under the influence of the endowment effect, there is the risk you are essentially overvaluing the worth of those stocks and have the potential of hanging onto a position perhaps longer than you should. The mere fact of ownership creates a psychological bias that those shares are "worth" more than other investment options.

There are many more examples of when you exert this behavior, but I am hoping at this point you are able to recognize how the endowment effect impacts your decision-making when it comes to managing your money.

The question is, what can we do about it? How do we short-circuit the endowment effect? There's no easy answer, but here are five Jedi mind tricks you can play on yourself to potentially reduce the impact:

**Actionable Step 1:**
*Let's start with awareness.* For anyone who is familiar with or has practiced mindfulness, you have gone through the process of viewing yourself from the outside in. It's also a desirable mental state that can help you overcome the power of the endowment effect. Mindfulness and meditation can potentially help you let go of the personal value you have given something and reduce its influence on you.

**Actionable Step 2:**
*Some creative thinking wouldn't hurt.* When you need to make financial decisions about savings, investing, borrowing or even expenses, imagine they are not yours. This can weaken their emotional influences. And this is a message for the know-it-

alls out there: How easy and confident do you feel when giving friends and family advice? But ask yourself, how effective are you at following the same advice as you would give others in a similar situation? As an example, do you know an expert in a given field that has told you to stay the course, but later learn they themselves did not? And I need to be honest, Despite all that I know about our behavior and money, I find myself falling into the same psychological traps as you do, even when I see it happening.

**Actionable Step 3:**

*Take out a notepad (or what I like to do is use a note-taking app on my smartphone).* List the purpose and potential benefits relating to the possession you are contemplating a financial decision. But go beyond the pros versus the cons. Change those columns to consider two other facets of the decision making process. In the first column, write WHY at the top. This is where you ask yourself what this solves for and jot down the responses. In the second column, write ALTERNATIVES/ CONSEQUENCES at the top. In this column write down any options that can satisfy the same need or intent, based on your current situation, or what you will be giving up if you maintain this "possession." This exercise narrows the gap between the value we have given to something vs. its value in terms of its true benefit. This will help improve your ability to compare the value to those items you do not own.

**Actionable Step 4:**
*Untether the connections.* When it comes to our money, we are often swayed by the ownership of investments or items where we have forged emotional connections. A variation to the column comparison just mentioned, is to do the homework assignment all over again. What I mean by this is to go through the financial-decision process as if you do not own the item in question to reduce biases. For example, let's say you have an investment you are deciding whether to keep or sell. Take the approach as if you don't have that need or want in your possession today. This helps you hit the reset button to establish the worth of an investment today and potential for the future versus looking through a rear view mirror and contemplating the value you reaped from owning it up to this point.

**Actionable Step 5:**
*Remove barriers.* Another option and methodology is to reduce the psychological roadblocks we build that prevent us from taking the appropriate action. This relates to opposing forces of motivators versus demotivators and our perceptions and aptitude to take action that leads to change. That was a mouthful. So let me explain with an example: I'll use the desire

to own a new home. To trigger this aspiration, you've apparently built a list of welcoming outcomes that would result from owning a new home. Could be from discussions with your significant other or growing family needs, maybe it is a more desirable neighborhood, job opportunities, etc.

Regardless, we get excited by the idea of a positive change in our lives, we go online and start perusing available homes. Then we visualize ourselves living in those homes and it further drives our motivation. But here is where the endowment effect takes hold and we start creating demotivators that in turn inflate the value of staying in your current residence and create the perception that taking action is too hard. This includes the selling of an existing home, the possibility of having to shop and apply for a mortgage, the labor and the stress of moving, the unfamiliarity of a new community, and you will even sabotage your own pursuits by finding fault with each new home you consider. The barriers continue to rise, which add pain and fear and denial into the decision-making process. Soon it becomes easier to justify the home you are in today because the alternative seems very hard to do. To enable a more balanced decision, first become more knowledgeable about those demotivators, take the mystery out of the "what if's" of each and weaken their hold on you.

This technique may help you make more informed decisions when comparing the pros and cons of other, similar decisions such as starting a new business, contemplating a puppy for the family, dedicating time to a new hobby, exploring volunteer work, or considering a career opportunity.

By now, you may have recognized a common theme: Distancing yourself from ownership as part of the solution. It's one of the best ways to reduce the endowment effect and its power over you.

---

**Quick Bonus Tip**

When it comes to your investments within your portfolio, there's an old saying to cut the losers loose and let the winners run. That's easier said than done because of your emotional attachments to what you already own. However, if you are able to distance ownership and compare those same investments to alternatives available today, ask yourself which best satisfies your portfolio strategy and financial planning.

---

One last tidbit to ponder: The next time your ball goes over the fence and in a place that makes it difficult to repossess it or will require a great deal of energy to maintain it ...think to yourself...am I placing too much value on that ball?

# Chapter Three: Riddle Me This
## Key behavior: Mental Accounting

*There's a classic brain teaser that goes something like this: You're a farmer and you have with you a fox, a chicken and a bushel of corn. And you come across this river and you need to take these items across the river, but the boat that you are using can only hold a certain capacity of weight, which means you can only take each of these items across one at a time. So if you take the fox over first, the chicken is going to eat the corn. Take the corn over first, the fox is going to eat the chicken. And even if you bring the chicken over first, you still have to go back and forth and one may eat the other.*
*If you can solve this classic puzzle, you may learn that reaching your retirement goals is a similar riddle.*

I have a concession to make. I love brain teasers—crosswords and sudoku are okay, but I really love brain teasers such as the one you just read. The kind that forces you to think outside of the box and that short circuits your linear logic. What makes them so entertaining is that they push you to re-examine and reconstruct the way you approach a problem or challenge in order to arrive at the most fitting solution.

The reason I am discussing brain teasers and starting with a riddle is because it ties into this chapter's topic, which is **Mental Accounting**, a concept introduced by Richard Thaler in 1985.[6] This is when you utilize a line of thinking that appears to make sense, but is actually sub-optimal and can potentially lead to self-destructive habits or poor decisions. It's a concern because mental accounting can generate misleading validations of your financial decision-making and result in the inefficient use of money, undermine a financial plan and potentially cheat you from achieving your long term goals.

We create mental buckets because they help us justify and compartmentalize the use of our money for assigned purposes. The best way to explain this phenomenon is with an illustration so picture this.

Picture this scenario from Thaler's 1999 research:[7] A concert or theatrical event is now playing in your area that you are really excited about seeing. And for the sake of this exercise, let's say you could not order in advance and had to pay in cash at the door. The price of admission is $100 per ticket. And so you head over to the theater and as the line you are waiting

---

[6] Thaler, R. H. (1985). Mental accounting and consumer choice. Marketing Science, 4(3), (pp. 199-214).

[7] Thaler, R. H. (1999). Mental accounting matters. Journal of Behavioral Decision Making, 12. (pp. 183-206)

on gets closer to the box office, you discover that you have lost the crisp $100 bill in your wallet you were going to use to pay for that ticket. My question to you: Are you still willing to pay $100 for a ticket? Try not to contemplate your answer and take a quick mental note of a simple yes or no to the question.

Now let's modify the scenario. Let's say you successfully bought a ticket and with a physical stub in hand, you head over to the theater entrance and wait in the line. However, when you get to the door, you discover that you have lost the ticket and you are unable to get a replacement. Now may I ask: Would you pay $100 at the box office for another ticket or skip the show?

In both ordeals, $100 is irretrievably lost whether in the form of cash or a ticket, but you are forced to consider whether or not the concert or theater experience is worth paying another $100. The response logically should not change, but when a study was conducted with a similar scenario using an admission price of $10, the answers actually do change by a significant margin. Respondents to the first scenario where cash is lost, 88% said they would buy another ticket, yet in the second scenario, 55% said they would NOT purchase a replacement. Please note I changed the value of the tickets from $10 to $100 for the purposes of bringing the illustration in line with today's costs, but the tugging in your brain over the two problems should be relatively the same.

So what's going on inside our brain?

Let's start with the latter scenario first, where we pre-purchased the ticket. Our minds created a mental bucket and gave the money a purpose for the entertainment expected. If all went well and we had the pleasure of experiencing the show, the assigned use of the money would have been satisfied. But when we had to pay for another ticket, that reopens the dedicated entertainment bucket and now appears as though we are paying double for the same purpose, which many might find too high a price to pursue. Why? Because we used up the money established for the purpose.

Now if we return to the first scenario where we lost the physical cash, there is no mental bucket associated with the $100. Yes, in all likelihood we are upset about the missing money, but that loss is not linked to the actual entertainment, and that's why it makes it easier and more probable you will consider purchasing another ticket.

These buckets, in terms of mental accounting, build on this cognitive thinking of organizing, evaluating and keeping track of financial activities. Here is how the process works: You assign a bucket into various silos you deem of value. Often, it's in terms of expenditures such as groceries, housing, entertainment, vacations, utilities, restaurants and bars, car-related costs like gas ... you get the idea. The intentions are good. They are set up to help you manage your money, but it forces you to treat the money differently depending on its assigned purpose.

Here's another illustration which conveys the power of mental accounting. Do you treat money differently when it's a tax refund, or how about birthday money, or speculative investments not part of your normal investing activity? I know many intelligent people in my life who have very comprehensive financial plans, yet bring up the topic of bonuses and they will tell you all sorts of creative ways they plan on spending that "additional" income.

I've got a great case in point. Have you ever been to a casino? If you ever played a betting game and were winning more than you were losing...that's awesome. But what do we call that money when you are up? That's right—you're playing with the "dealers or casinos money," and chances are you are going to treat that money differently, which may lead to more risky behavior.

The funny thing is when it comes to mental accounting, sometimes a $1 does not equal a $1. Let me explain. Picture you are on the hunt for new furniture, let's say a table, and you found the perfect one in a furniture showroom near your home for $200. However, if you learn that it is only $180 at a different furniture store 20 minutes down the road, you would probably travel a little further to save 10% off the price. But what if you were seeking to replace your entire living room with a complete ensemble of furniture that included three tables, a couch and chair. The local furniture showroom is selling the set for $2,000. Meanwhile the furniture store 20 minutes down the road that we mentioned previously is selling the same set for $1,980. Would you drive to save a mere 1% less?

It doesn't sound worth the effort, but in both cases the amount you would save is $20. Why did we discount the cash when it was for a larger purchase? That's because we assigned a different value to the savings in relation to the price.

Anyone who has ever been involved with the purchase of a sizable vacation package can easily be wooed to upgrade their hotel rooms, excursions, or airplane seats for just a few hundred dollars more. But shrink the size of the vacation and those few dollars more to spend on perks seem less valuable for what you would be receiving in return.

Mental accounting works in the opposite direction as well. An offshoot of this is the *sunk cost fallacy*, which is when your behavior is driven by the resources already committed to a decision. This is when you feel compelled to continue the pursuit of repetitive or particular activities to justify the time, money or effort you have already invested.

Need an example? I love giving examples and of course I have one: memberships. I'm talking about memberships to the gym, a class, a wine club, a book club, warehouse clubs, cosmetic clubs, community clubs or even those ever-popular, direct-to-home meal clubs. In each case, you have made some form of commitment by signing up and to get the most from your personal investment, you feel compelled to attempt to use them more.

I have another form of club that I am guessing you can relate to and that's loyalty clubs. Have you ever felt compelled to purchase up to 5 or 10 or more of a product or service, or some established dollar amount just to receive some type of reward for free?

If you are a Seinfeld fan, you might recall an episode where Elaine is super excited about completing her loyalty card to a sandwich shop. In order to receive a free sandwich, she purchased 10 subs to get one free. Inadvertently, she uses the completed loyalty card to write down a fake phone number, and mistakenly gives it to this guy she is not really interested in dating. Part of the humor is watching her go to all sorts of extremes to track him down so she can get her free sub.

But, I'm just as guilty. I cannot tell you how much I was driven a few years ago by a promotion to spend a certain dollar amount at the shops at Grand Central Station in New York CIty in order to receive an inexpensive backpack that said Grand Central on it. Looking back, that was some real wonky mental accounting I did to justify the reward.

But before you laugh at me, I bet I can make you laugh at yourself too. Are you going to tell me there wasn't a time where you were tempted by a tasty piece of pie or gooey chocolate chip cookie or scrumptious slice of cake or how about that pint of salted caramel ice cream, and then you caved in and ate it? Oh yum. Thereafter, you probably justified eating it through your own mental bucketing system by creating one labeled calorie cap for the day. So based on this logical (or rather illogical) thinking, you probably told yourself: that's ok, I'll just skip lunch or dinner and it all balances out. Yet you know darn well the nutritional comparisons are completely uncomparable.

This can also be witnessed when it comes to convenient excuses and justifications for not working out. Maybe you can forgo the exercise routine because walking the dog three times today counts. Or, maybe you equate exercise with being physically active while doing house chores. And then there is the weather—it was too hot, too cold or too gloomy today.

Let's go back to the sweets and perhaps you discount exercising for today because you reduce your calorie intake by not eating the ice cream, which justifies delaying exercising for tomorrow. Look, I'm not saying that walking an additional few steps or avoiding sweets don't count, but they definitely do not derive the same benefit as a dedicated workout.

Hopefully you clearly see the behavioral risks involved with this line of thinking. So let's get back to mental accounting as it relates to your finances.

Earlier I mentioned silos and how you create buckets for different purposes such as your day-to-day expenses. But you need to be aware those purposes are more constructs of our brain versus actual accounting. Unless you literally have separate accounts at the bank for all these various financial activities. However, you may be asking: "What's wrong with the bucket list, sounds to me like a great way to maintain a budget." Well, the issue with this approach is the lack of important parameters that consider needs versus wants and short-term versus long-term goals. It's like arbitrarily assigning the value of the use of money equally to paying your monthly utilities as allocating money to a vacation or saving for retirement.

But it's not all bad. Mental accounting can be your friend or foe depending on how you apply it to your decision-making process.

**Actionable Step 1:**
*Establish a systematic savings or investment program.* This encourages you to allocate a portion of your paycheck for an important purpose. The key is to determine the affordable

contribution you can make without creating a shortage for essential needs and other desirable goals.

**Actionable Step 2:**
*Expect the unexpected.* Another commonly mentioned and healthy bucket is establishing an emergency fund to help reduce the impact of the unexpected.

**Actionable Step 3:**
*Consider the appropriate buckets.* I have also seen mental accounting solely used to the advantage of retirement planning via three buckets: Early retirement, late retirement and legacy. That is another great example of how to create healthy financial wellness.

But these are just remnants of the bigger picture. Remember earlier I mentioned the importance of particular, evaluative parameters that included needs vs. wants as well as defining the time horizon of various desires you are seeking to fulfill in your life.

I was not expecting to plug a book this episode, but I found the process offered in a book entitled, Worry-free money,[8] written by Shannon Lee Simmons, a compelling argument for the use of buckets when done right even though it is uncertain

---

[8] Simmons, Shannon Lee. Worry-Free Money: The guilt-free approach to managing your money and your life. Collins. December 2017.

whether the author had mental accounting in mind, but what follows is the concept:

**Actionable Step 5:**
*Establish buckets into more broadly and meaningful categories.* The first one contains fixed expenses such as utility bills, rent, mortgage and the like, and two additional buckets for short-term goals like a vacation or new furniture or an emergency fund and long-term goals like contributions toward retirement. You need to do a bit of math to determine the time horizons and how much you need to put away monthly to reach the longer-term goals, but what remains in a fourth bucket is your spending money.

Why I like this concept is it helps overcome an important emotion, and that's guilt. As long as you do not overspend what is in that last bucket, you should be able to spend that money anyway you desire whether it's that fancy cappuccino, new clothes, an impulsive buy online or that show for $100. The feelings of awkwardness or a sense of shame for spending the money for such things is significantly reduced. Why? Because you have paid yourself first, you took care of the financial obligations associated with what you need today and what you want tomorrow.

This chapter was all about turning the mental accounting concept from a behavioral risk to a behavioral strength, and this can be done by recognizing how you distribute the use of your money once earned. The intent may be to save more, invest in a goals-based asset allocation strategy or paying down loans quicker, but the true value is what you gain from those financial activities in terms of improved financial wellness.

I think it is time we return to the riddle that was provided at the start of this chapter, but I would like you to swap out the Chicken for needs, the corn for wants and the fox for the unexpected expenses. And it makes it easier to see how important it is to maintain an eye on your needs, feed your wants and desires, while taking steps to reduce the impact of the unplanned. If you solved the riddle, the balancing act I just described between the three makes sense.

But If you are having difficulties seeking a solution for our farmer in distress, I won't leave you hanging. It goes like this. Take the chicken across the river first; go back for the fox; drop the fox off after crossing the river, but pick back up the chicken and place it back into the boat, leaving the fox alone. At this point, you can return to the other shore, drop off the chicken and grab the corn; take the corn to the side where the fox is, and then go back for the chicken.

# Chapter Four: Early Temptations
## Key behavior: Delayed Gratification

*Between the years of 1968 and 1977, over 550 preschoolers were each placed into a room with only a chair and a table—and on that table sat one glorious, sweet tasting marshmallow. Each child was given the option to eat the treat, or if they could wait, for an unspecified amount of time, would receive another two marshmallows.*

*The results of this self-control experiment are interesting ... but I'm wondering ... would you have been able to hold out for more marshmallows?*

I have always been fascinated by this test and its predictive implications for many years. We'll get into the details of the marshmallow test shortly. But I'd like to set the stage first.

Back in the Introduction of this book, I mentioned our ongoing desire to make positive changes in our lives and cited a few examples of our daily challenges such as exercising more, getting trim, quitting the tobacco habit, the wooing of a holiday sale—and of course New Year's resolutions. To overcome any of these challenges, it takes willpower and your ability to exert self-restraint.

What I'm leading to is the concept and benefits of **Delayed Gratification.** Just like those times when you save up for something you want or a long-term investment strategy. In a more overarching sense, it's holding out for something better or something promised or a commitment with the belief that doing so will earn you a specific reward.

Delayed gratification is more than an indicator of one's ability to attain long term goals, it also helps build empathy, listening skills, and patience which are essential ingredients in forging positive relationships. And what I'd like to do is help you forge a more positive relationship with your money.

If you choose to conduct a search on the web about delayed gratification, you'll find an overwhelming number of links and references to Walther Michel and his colleague's groundbreaking study of the Marshmallow Test conducted in the early 70s.[9] Walter Mischel's intent was to determine if there was a correlation to how long a preschooler would wait for a marshmallow could help predict any long-term consequential life outcomes.

For accurate measure, the description in the intro teaser at the start of this chapter was one of several experiments. Other

---

[9] Mischel, Walter. The Marshmallow Test: Mastering Self-Control. Little, Brown Spark. September 2014.

experiments included different types of stimuli and props available for distractors to help with avoiding temptations. To be specific: The children were tempted by a reward that an instructor introduced to them, and if they could avoid eating or taking that reward, while the instructor was out of the room for a duration of 15 minutes, they would double that reward. If temptation was too great, they could have what was given to them and notify the instructor of their decision by ringing a bell that also sat upon the table.

The intent of this research was to create conditions that facilitate self-control, determine what undermines it, and potentially help those who show deficiencies in it, ways to escape from being a victim of this behavior. The study was also repeated in the 80's and 90's, where the preschoolers were tracked through adolescence to early adulthood.

What was central to the research was this concept of our hot system, which feeds immediate rewards, versus our cool system that permits us to delay rewards. It's important to state that one system is not necessarily better than the other, both are necessary. The hot cognition is often automatic, rapid and led by our emotions. Think in terms of jumping out of the way of a car that has accidentally veered in your direction or comforting someone who is sad, or laughing at a joke. Cold cognition is often considered independent from your emotional thinking and associated with logic and critical thinking. Think weighting of probabilities and outcomes based on known facts. It's tempting to desire to be cold, cognitive thinkers, but be wary. Decisions utilizing strictly the cold system often lead to no gain or loss by achieving those tasks, which means there is a lack of feelings toward the results. This could also lead to a lack of empathy as well. It is what troubles me when I hear the media and advice trying to convince you to take the emotions out of your decision-making process. In the end, all decisions have an emotional element to them.

In reality, we are human, fallible, thrive on emotional stimuli...and why I say it is better to focus on how to better accommodate your emotions into your thinking. Those emotions are the spice of life. Now that we established that emotions are part of the decision-making process, we can go back to delayed gratification and the marshmallow test.

## CAN I TRUST YOU?

There is an underlying component to delayed gratification that I feel is often missed in research and articles about the subject matter—and that's trust. Whether that's trust in the promise made by a person, by an organization, or to yourself. The pursuit of your desire to delay gratification is tethered to trust and the belief that what you can achieve tomorrow is better than what you have today.

It's when we expect someone or something to arrive on time, when we question the quality of a product or service bought

> online or in a brick-and-mortar store, the reliability of public transportation, counting on public services to clean the roads after a major winter storm, that my spouse expects me to pick up her favorite pint of vanilla ice cream at the grocery store...and let me tell you...that's a marriage-breaker if I fail at that trusted task. I am going off on a tangent here, but in each situation delayed gratification must be observed to achieve or obtain more desirable results than doing something today.

One aspect of the Marshmallow Test is that in later repeated studies, the preschoolers were evaluated 12 years later when they were in their twenties. At this point, It may not surprise you that those innocent young children who were able to hold out and not eat that tasty little morsel in front of them all those years ago exhibited as adults more self-control in frustrating situations, yielded less to temptation, were able to hold their concentration, obtained a higher education, were deemed more intelligent, self-reliant, confident, and trusted their own judgment.

In addition, those who delayed gratification scored higher when it came to planning and staying the course when pursuing their goals. I would gather that translates into improved financial decision making and outcomes as well.

To be balanced, there has been more recent research conducted that has attempted to poke holes in the Marshmallow Test. As an example, there are other facets that need to be considered in terms of one's ability to delay gratification—acknowledging one's social and economic background. This may include the makeup of one's household, income and education levels. And some children have had previous experience with adults who don't keep their word. Imagine that!

So, when locked up in a room and an adult is telling them: "Hey Sally, you can eat this marshmallow now if you want, but if you can hold out for 15 minutes until I come back, I'll give you another one. Leaving you with two marshmallows." Some kids have learned painful, worldly lessons and have experienced adults who either failed to keep promises or experienced poor outcomes when there was a lack of fairness. Leading some children to recognize that if you have something good, someone may end up taking it away if you wait.

This leads to the concept of over promissory statements and expectations. For example, what about promised results when taking ginseng to improve your memory, taking vitamin C to avoid a cold, or if you walk 10,000 steps a day, you'll lose weight. The key phrase that needs insertion is "helps you." Ginseng *helps you* improve your memory, vitamin C *helps you* avoid a cold, and when I started walking 10,000 steps a day...it *helped me* lose the weight, but it was not walking the steps alone. It was a combination of other factors such as an improved diet and exercising more. If you say no to dessert tonight (or a marshmallow), you are not going to wake up five pounds thinner in the morning, but you may wake up thinner than you were.

It's about setting realistic expectations. So when we look at delayed gratification, it does not necessarily mean, as an example, that if you invest your money today instead of satisfying some more immediate desire, that you'll definitely reach your retirement goals, but it can *help* to be one of several contributing factors.

All that being said, I would definitely not discount the value of any foundational study. Anyone who is familiar with conducting research knows also that the fewer variables you enter into the equation, the more likely you are able to find your conclusions useful. And the Marshmallow test has some useful and valuable conclusions. So with expectations established, let's get into the benefits of delayed gratification where it can be a force of good for you and your money, which include:

- The probabilities of saving more and borrowing less. Such as planning to buy those new clothes or new phone vs. leveraging credit card debt
- The ability to find the right balance of cost and benefit when it comes to funding education or buying a new home
- The ability to generate a nice nest egg for retirement
- Often the purpose behind buying a life insurance policy or an annuity

## EXPLAINING ANNUITIES

Annuities are an often-misunderstood financial product for the benefit of your retirement. They may or may not be the right financial option for you, and there are various types depending on your individual financial objectives and goals. So, let's take a detour from the conversation of this chapter to help you make a more informed decision about annuities.

Annuities are normally a guarantee by a financial institution to promise to provide an often-fixed payout for a specified period of time or for the rest of your life, based on the purchase price of the annuity and your own life expectancy. First and foremost, they are not an investment, they are a purchase. I start with this because one of the most common misconceptions is to compare the purchase price of an annuity, say for $100,000 with a monthly payout of $500 per month at age 65 versus an investment in equities that may get you an average rate of about 10% a year. All these numbers are for illustrative purposes and may actually be higher or lower depending on the age you start payout or when you started investing, but bear with me.

From a time and investment perspective you may make more from investing in the market, but it's the wrong psychology being applied. Investing is often part of the accumulation phase of your lifetime, whereas an annuity is concerned with the income distribution period, or retirement phase of your life. They are apples and oranges. One is for accumulating wealth, whereas the annuities are all about establishing guaranteed income streams.

Let me further illustrate this. We all pay social security taxes right? You see it on your pay stubs and W-2s. But ask yourself, do you know how much you have paid into social security over the years? Have you ever thought what you could do with that money if you invested it into the market? Probably not and why is that? It's because of how you view Social Security. Most Americans see it as the money the government is going to pay us monthly when we retire. You don't look at it in terms of wealth building, you look at it as retirement income. But in reality, Social Security is probably one of the largest annuity programs in the world!

Let's wrap up this discussion of this chapter with some useful tips how to build delayed gratification:

**Actionable Step 1:**
*Avoid exposure to the actual reward.* However an image or a reminder of the reward to illustrate what you will get if you wait can be beneficial. In the Marshmallow Test, preschoolers fared twice as well when they were exposed to a picture of the reward in front of them as a reminder. So, if you are trying to save for that vacation to Tahiti, put up that picture of the

island on your refrigerator as a daily reminder to curb the frivolous spending—it works.

**Actionable Step 2:**
*Have more than one strategy for known situations or desires of temptation.* It was found that those who understood strategies to delay gratification are able to wait longer. What's important to note is it is not IF you will be tempted, but getting into the mindset of WHEN you will be tempted that triggers appropriate planning to curb temptations.

### A TALE OF TEMPTATION

I found temptation a very prevalent theme in Homer's epic classic, the Odyssey. For those who may be unfamiliar or just a refresher...it's about Odysseus, a king who presided over a small island in Greece named Ithaca. He sets off to sea to fight in the Trojan War, but he and his crew face many temptations. Some that they were able to overcome and some that they simply could not resist. But one of the most well-known temptations in the Odyssey was when they had to overcome the wooing of the Sirens that were of many men their doom. These were enchanting mermaids, who lured nearby sailors with their music and singing voices while having to cause shipwrecks on the rocky coast of the island of which they presided. Knowing of the potential temptations, Odysseus had a strategy to overcome the lure of the Sirens. He had his crew plug their ears with beeswax

> and tied him to the ship so he could not be wooed by the Sirens' song. The Odyssey is riddled with many learning lessons about willpower and delayed gratification.

**Actionable Step 3:**

*Focus on the greater outcome versus the immediate experience.* Going back to the Marshmallow Test, If you focus on anticipating the chewy, sweet taste of the marshmallows versus the accumulation or improved outcome of the reward, chances are your willpower will cave. Better to focus on the potential for measured results than the immediate satisfaction.

**Actionable Step 4:**

*Imagine how someone reasonable would behave.* Interestingly enough, if you envision having to choose for someone else in a similar situation you are more willing to select delayed gratification as you would choose for yourself. There are times we already subconsciously do this in situations where we are at a crossroads and think of someone we look up to as a role model and say "what would our hero do in this situation?" Transferring the decision from your perspective to someone else's can help you avoid immediate temptation.

In Chapter 3, we discussed budgeting and mental accounting. If there is something that you wish to attain, make sure to add to the short-term or long-term bucket that would force you to stash money away for that purpose and thereby reduce your discretionary spending bucket accordingly. This also may help place a longer-term perspective on what you perceive as short-term rewards, and thus realistically place desired goals into the appropriate buckets.

**Actionable Step 5:**

*Move from hot to cool responses.* Turn short-term rewards into future rewards so you'll be able to more easily recognize the monetary impact. I think this requires a few examples. Do you have digital subscriptions to online publications, streaming video or some other media resource? Often the seller of services will offer an affordable pitch such as for around $3.33 a day, you'll gain access to over 500 channels to explore movies, tv shows and more. That sounds great—where do I sign up! However, annualize that expense and ask yourself do you feel any hesitation giving up $1,200 a year (oh and plus all kinds of taxes and fees)? It's the same monetary value, but visualizing the cumulative value can cool your hot response to the immediate rewards.

If there is a mantra to remind yourself, it's that early temptations predict future expectations. And if I had to confess, especially with the sweet tooth I have, I fear that I would have failed the Marshmallow Test as a preschooler. It's probably what has driven me to focus on behavior economics and that led me to a career of helping others improve their financial literacy.

# Chapter Five: Needs And Nickels
## Key behavior: Human Motivation Theory

*How would you like to learn more about the ways you exert control? If you're interested, have I got a fun activity for you. I'd like for you and a few friends or adult family members to conduct an auction. But what makes this auction a little unusual is that you have an opportunity to bid on five nickels one at a time.*

*Now it may sound a little strange, but nevertheless you are about to engage in a bidding war for those nickels. And believe it or not, this exercise can help discover the types of needs you have and how you behave to satisfy those needs.*

In this chapter, I am going to ask you to exercise your brain. But let's have a little chat first about our general need for control, or possibly the lack thereof, as it relates to our emotions.

The ability to control your environment dictates the level of positive inferences, happiness and satisfaction you have with a particular event, activity, possessions and people. What's interesting is we all want control, but how we gain a sense of control is triggered by our individual needs. And it's not which needs are necessarily better at obtaining control, rather it's which needs help you achieve the highest level of satisfaction.

So before we take a deep dive into the subject matter, it's time I walk you through a fun exercise. Get ready! You and I are going to have a friendly little auction for five imaginary nickels. Now for background, I learned about this engaging experiment in my understudies (which of course was a lifetime ago), when I first learned about organizational psychology. And to this day, and on occasion, I take this test out of my mental pocket during private gatherings—just to liven up the party.

As we go through this exercise, I ask that you be a little patient because conducting this game via words on a page versus in-person is a tad tricky. So first, take a moment and clear your head. I will need you to dedicate the next minute or two to the task at hand.

It's time to put on your visual thinking cap. Picture me and you sitting across from each other at a table. In the center of the table sits five nickels. Actually, there should be five props that look like or represent nickels and not the real thing. If it makes it easier, picture five nickels made out of cardboard. Have that image in your head? Good, because you and I are going to bid for each of those nickels—one at a time.

Now keep in mind this is pretend play and they are five items that represent nickels, but not the actual money. It's kind of like playing with poker chips. The bidding will start at one cent and in terms of maximum bid, the sky's the limit! And let me preface and assure you that there is no right or wrong response to your bidding behavior. Ready? Here we go:

AUCTION 1: I'll start the bidding at one cent. Will you bid more than one cent? How about two cents, what if I come back and say three cents....will you let me have it for three or will you up the ante to four cents? What if I say five, will you go up to six cents? I now bid seven, will you take it even higher? Make note of who won each auction and at what price.

*Now let's move on to the next round.*

AUCTION 2: So if I started last time, it's your turn to begin the bidding at one cent. And let's say I jump right to a response of four cents. Will you stop the auction now and let me have it for that amount or are you going to respond higher? How much higher? Have you set a limit to how high you are willing to go regardless who wins? Or knowing you are not playing with real money, is there no stopping you until you win that imaginary nickel?

This continues until you have completed five auctions.

*I think you get the idea. Now that you know how the auction works, PUT DOWN THE BOOK and conduct a round of auctions with no less than two other people until you have completed the bidding process for all five nickels. Again, make sure to keep notes of the outcomes of the auctions; it's pivotal to the discovery process.*

So, let's be honest ... you aren't going to put down the book and do this activity right now are you? I knew it! That's ok. The lessons here will not be lost, but you may have difficulty determining your true self should you choose to play out the full rounds of the game at a later time. We are such impatient creatures are we not?

So, tell me: How many times do you THINK you would let the other person have the nickel for a lower value? How many times would you keep bidding to win the auction? Or, are you someone who had a specific value or strategy in mind and consequently stuck with that particular strategy regardless if you won or lost a particular auction?

I'll explain how this auction plugs into this chapter's discussion shortly, but first, let's get into the history of this activity and its purpose so as to not lead you into thinking this is some absurd game to simply play on your emotions.

David McClelland, who passed away in 1998, was a brilliant American psychologist. David published numerous papers on Needs Theory during the 1950s thru 1990s.[10] And his findings

---

[10] McClelland, David. The Achieving Society. Simon and Schuster. 1961.

and work were aptly named the **Expected Theory of Motivation,** which states that each and every one of us has a compelling driving motivator.

The source of your motivation falls into the following three categories: And they are Achievement, Affiliation and Power. Let's discuss what characterizes each of these needs.

NEEDS CATEGORY 1: People with a higher need for **achievement** strive for challenges, like to attain goals and expect to receive praise for their accomplishments. These are problem-solvers and often enjoy working alone or with others with a similar drive.

NEEDS CATEGORY 2: People with a higher need for **affiliation** like to be part of the group. They are less interested in praise and more about the camaraderie, teamwork and relationships that are forged. They also tend to be more risk averse, but care greatly for those in their group.

NEEDS CATEGORY 3: People with a higher need for **power** like to take charge of situations, thrive on competition, be seen as leaders and expect to be widely recognized for their efforts. They often need motivators and are often capable of motivating others. They are also highly effective negotiators. These are the leaders of a team, a business unit or organization, or even your home (regardless if the title "head of household" is placed on you or not).

The nickels auction, while not always 100% accurate, is a useful tool to discover the need or needs that motivate you and that you use to *exert control*. Before we get into analyzing the outcomes, I'd like to reiterate that we have taken a shortcut to the process by not actually conducting the bidding activity. Therefore, I am asking how you think you would react versus actual, observed responses. When time permits and for a little fun, introduce the nickels auction with a few friends and adult family members to obtain a true response, but do not explain the different needs until thereafter.

So during the auction, if you are someone who lets the other bidder win the round, usually for less than five cents, you may have a higher need for *affiliation*. That's because it makes you feel good when another person experiences the win. I have seen participants with this trait even let someone win the nickel at the opening bid for one cent!

If you are someone who was determined to win, chances are you kept raising the stakes until you gained possession of that nickel. Why not, it's imaginary. If you fit this description, you have a high need for *power*. I have witnessed those with a need for power go over $5 and more for that nickel!

And finally, if you are someone who has established a goal, such as telling yourself the nickel is worth five cents and I am willing to pay up to that amount and no more, regardless if I win or lose—then you have a high need for *achievement*. By the way, the goal could be any amount or the goal could have been a desire to win 3 out of 5 auctions, etc. People with this trait sometimes are perplexed in trying to determine the logic of the experiment.

The auction is entertaining in its own right, but put two people of the same needs category together in a bidding war and it gets quite amusing. Two bidders with a need for affiliation, and they wrap up the experiment fairly quickly because there are less bidding rounds and they just seem so happy to have played. Two bidders with a need for power, and watch the battle. I've had to intervene with these situations sometimes because the value of that nickel becomes astronomical. They take winning seriously.

Two people with a need for achievement tend to have a sense of satisfaction regardless of win or lose, but are more concerned with maintaining their chosen strategies. It's kind of funny because I sometimes see them sitting there shrugging their shoulders during the game. That's because they are somewhat on auto-pilot and cannot see the purpose of the auction. They are wondering why someone would not just follow the same set strategy every time.

So which needs category did you think you fall into? By the way, it is possible to have a major need and a minor need at work, but not all three are implemented to exert control. Now that you hopefully know your strongest need, you can use that as a strength when managing your money. What you are about to learn is your preferences drive your feelings and ability to exert control.

As an example, let's say three different people invested in the same stock with a purchase price of $100 a share. A year later it increased in value to $200 a share.

Someone with a need for power, may feel very satisfied because their investments outperformed an average investor by a wide margin and that person ranked higher than others in terms of their prowess with money. Someone with a need for achievement, may be very satisfied because the growth of the stock surpassed the targeted expectations and yearly goals in terms of performance. And someone with a need for affiliation, well they feel good about themselves because they are part of a group of investors who saw the same opportunity and are likely to share their success or experience in the forms of social media and conversation with others or perhaps even walk others through their investment strategy via storytelling.

However, these needs do not always dictate the benefits of a given object of desire. For example, you might associate philanthropy as a pursuit associated with people having a high need for affiliation because of their sharing nature. But anybody may desire to give to a charity, just the purpose and commitment are different. So where charitable giving in general strikes a chord with those with a need for affiliation, someone with a need for power, may see purpose to become a champion of its cause. Someone with a need for achievement may have a fixed, annual budget established to donate to charity to do their part. Regardless of the need, they all support philanthropy.

The overarching point I'm trying to make—it's about point of view. The benefits associated with a particular investment, event, activity, possession or personal relationship may be the same, but the satisfaction derived from the association may vary. So, purpose is part of your way of exerting control over your financial decision-making.

### WHO'S COMING TO THE PARTY?

These needs motivations playout in our everyday lives. Tell me if you have not been in the following situation: Let's say you and your friends or perhaps your significant other are in a heated discussion as to whether or not to attend a particular social event (virtually or in-person). If you have, then the following questions and dialogue sound familiar to you. "Who is going to be there?" "Where is it going to be?" "How long is the event?" "How long do we have to stay?"

These inquiries sound innocent enough, but you better take cover! Because the answer for each question may be factual, but each will lead to a different emotional response based on your motivational needs. To illustrate, you may be asking who is going? And you say, "Mindy is going to be there." And the response you receive in return is, "Will she be coming with Pete?" And then you counter, "Of course she is coming with

Pete, who else would she come with?" Then the counter-statement could be, "I was just curious." Now you feel compelled to probe by asking, "Why then does it matter?!"

For someone with a need for affiliation, they may feel Pete does not add or opposingly adds a great deal of value to the social gathering. For someone with a need for power, they may feel competitive with Pete and want to prepare to win him over on any number of points depending on various subject matter. For someone with a need for achievement, this may be knowing Pete could be an important person to network with and you are strategizing how to engage Pete on the topic of career opportunities as an example.

The following are helpful tips based on needs category:

**NEED FOR AFFILIATION:**
Achievers often take calculated decisions and tend to have a low risk tolerance. If you fall into this category, it may be best to try and avoid having to make any quick decisions about your money. You are someone who probably likes to conduct a great deal of research and comb the web for additional facts, pros and cons before making that expenditure or investment. But this can also lead into other behavioral risks such as confirmation bias, which is mentally weighing toward your favored opinions. *On a side note: I am someone who seeks achievement... and the amount of hours, if not days, I invest into*

*researching is truly cringe-worthy. So that's right, leave all the vacation planning to me.*

**NEED FOR POWER**

Empowerment-seekers often are self-disciplined, and acknowledge a zero sum game in which if you are winning, someone must be losing. Status, determination and recognition are important drivers. If they see an opportunity, they often jump on it and reap the rewards. They are often the first to try something new and others to follow. But be wary, empowerment-seekers may be prone to overconfidence in terms of a behavioral risk.

**NEED FOR AFFILIATION**

Affiliators like the sense of belonging and the ability to socialize experiences. Win or lose is not as important as the positive inferences resulting from a group decision. They also see it as best to play by the rules, or even bend the rules, but not break them. Fulfillment comes from making financial decisions that fit into a current culture or generally accepted norms. They gain strong insights and recommendations from the experiences and stories shared by others. However, they may at times be at risk of clouded judgment resulting from groupthink and herding behavior that come from reacting to a collective consciousness.

There are other motivation theories out there, such as Maslow's famous hierarchy of needs, but I feel McClelland's is more transferable in terms of financial decision making, organizational psychology and leadership. And why leadership? That's because you can swap out power with effectiveness, achievement with efficiency, and affiliation with empathy. And how do you judge someone with strong leadership skills? Is it not based on the same three characteristics? When we define someone as a good leader, we usually say it's because they know how to take charge of difficult situations, they are highly accomplished, or that they really understand people.

Before you go out there and start exerting control, I encourage you to gather with a few friends and family members and have yourself a fun, little auction to learn what a nickel is worth to you.

# Chapter Six: I've Been Framed
## Key behavior: Framing Effect

*Two friends decide to meet and go to an art museum. In particular, they choose to visit the Expressionists paintings because they have been informed that there is a copy of the famous Edvard Munch's The Scream on display. The two patrons spend a lengthy time observing the painting and see other exhibits at the museum as well.*

*Not long thereafter, they decide to stop at a local cafe for coffee and reflect on their recent visit to gallery, when one turns to the other and says..."How about The Scream..such a robust and exhilarating painting with its clever use of colors, the vibrant orange sky, the playful ghost-like shape of the figure and that startled face...so comical."*

*The fellow friend turns back and responds, "Were we looking at the same picture? My impression of the painting was a person under terrible stress, having a panic attack, and sharing a traumatic experience on the dock on which the figure stood."*

*Are either one incorrect in their evaluations?*

You've often heard of real-life or fictional stories where a crime has been committed, and there were several witnesses to the act of aggression. When the detectives interviewed each person to determine what happened, the individual interpretations of the criminal activity strangely sound as though each witnessed a different crime scene altogether.

It's an interesting phenomenon and how we tend to interpret a situation through limited information.

This leads to the focus of this chapter: **Framing Effects** and cognitive biases, which is when we make decisions based on the way information is presented to us. The facts may be the same, but how those facts are shared, or seen through a limited scope, influence our decision-making process. Back in chapter one, we talked about heuristics and how we use short-cuts in our mind to make choices and judgements. Framing effects can short-circuit those short-cuts.

That's because framing limits our mental vision, just like when looking at a painting. The frame we are viewing can sway us to focus on particular elements of an image—whether that's color, historical perspective, or what we are allowed to see based on the constraints of its own borders.

And speaking of Sway,[11] there is a book with the same name that was released back in 2008 by the brothers Ori and Rom

---

[11] Brafman, Ori and Brafman, Rom. Sway: The Irresistible Pull of Irrational Behavior. Currency. June 2008.

Brafman. I mention the book because it particularly discusses attribution bias, which is our tendency to make decisions based on *perceived value* versus *objective facts*. This means we are highly susceptible to how a product, service or situation is presented to us. And it's those influences that create cognitive bias.

> **THE BLIND MEN AND THE ELEPHANT**
>
> There's an ancient tale that comes from the southeast-Asian region about a group of blind men who are informed that an elephant has been captured and currently held in the center of their town. None of these blind men have ever been in the physical presence of an elephant and so being curious, but unable to see, desire to do what they do best and that is to learn through touching.
>
> So, they journey to the center of town where this elephant is held in captivity and go forth to examine this extraordinary animal. But due to its enormous size each sightless individual approaches a different side and describes to one another the elephant based on their individual experience. And as a result, their descriptions greatly differ from one another.
>
> One touches the trunk and says it feels like a thick snake. The second blind man approaches its side and says it is nothing but a wall, the third reaches its legs and says it is like a tree, another touches its tail and says they are all wrong it is like a

> rope and yet another reaches for its tusk and claims it is a deadly weapon like a spear.
>
> The moral of the story is that one's subjective experience is limited by scope and we are influenced by what is presented to us. The failure to account for other facts and information, or seeing things through a narrow lens, is what short circuits those mental short cuts we use to make decisions.

Here are a few illustrative examples that may help you recognize how this framing effect is present in our everyday lives. Let's start with the grocery store because you are in the mood for a confectionary treat. When there, envision walking down the cookies aisle because, in particular, you are craving chocolate mint covered sandwich cookies (well, that's what I occasionally crave and of course you may have your own sweet tooth cravings).

While scanning the shelves, you see there are several choices, especially if you are seeking a low-fat option. And you spot two identical boxes with two similarly intended choices. One box label reads: 80% less fat than our original cookies. The label of the second box reads: only 20% fat of our original cookies.

Although they both offer the same benefit, I am guessing you will select the first box that has 80% less fat, because the way it is framed is more appealing to our senses. Now that example is fairly harmless, unless you ARE me and eat through a box of cookies regardless of its fat content. But all kidding aside, what if we are discussing more serious implications.

Think back to the last time you were in a competition whether it was a sport, a game with friends or family, a team project at work, or any form of rivalry where there is an us versus them mentality. So for the sake of an example, you and Jean are playing against one another in a friendly game of tennis with a few of your friends as spectators. And despite your skills and your ability to play the court, Jean scores higher than you. Upon the completion of the match, your spectator friends describe the outcome. How would you feel if they approached you and said, "Wow, You lost." What emotions does that evoke in you? What if instead they said, "Wow, Jean won!" It feels different doesn't it?!! Yet both statements are logically equivalent in terms of the outcome.

Any parents out there? Are you mindful of the way you state results of a competition your child was in? What if it was your child out on that tennis court and lost a match? I bet some of you have been involved with a college request for enrollment. If your child received a letter from the school communicating that unfortunately they were not selected, how did you respond? Did you say "well, it looks like you weren't good enough for that university" or did you say something like "it's unfortunate that the university failed to recognize your value,

I am sure others will." And by the way, what do we call those unfortunate letters from the college submission offices?—REJECTION letters! Maybe we need to relabel them as "Enrollment Selection" Status letters.

I think it's time we turn our attention to the impact of framing on our financial-decision making. Framing effects are incredibly influential in managing our money.

Perhaps a good place to begin is with credit cards. In your lifetime, have you ever accepted a credit card based on any of the following promotions: a zero percent offer? a balance transfer incentive? a cash back bonus on purchases? a tie-in to your favorite loyalty program? travel rewards? super enticing benefits? Depending on what sounds more alluring to your financial situation, these promotions are presented with a narrow lens.

If you were provided balanced information at the time the offer was presented, you may not be so triggered to accept these offers. No one is promoting the potential downsides of any offer unless you read the fine print. And even if you do, the framing of these perks without the tradeoffs has you focused only on the benefits promoted. In many cases, you may have witnessed the interest rate or annual fee increase to an astronomical number not longer after the promotional period ended?

Let's chat about a more sizable commitment like the financing of a new home. Primarily, you need to consider a fixed rate or an adjustable rate. Adjustable rates, also known as ARMs, can be very enticing when they are framed in terms of flexibility and the low rate you receive in the early year or years of a mortgage, despite the interest rate could creep up awfully high thereafter. Maybe that's not for you and prefer a fixed rate. If so, were you more convinced by the framing of a fixed rate with no points down or were you convinced to pay points up front to reduce that rate? I am not at liberty to say one is better than the other, but I can tell you how each of these options may have been introduced to you, and may have long-lasting and potentially costly repercussions to your financial health.

Perhaps you are someone who systematically puts money away into a savings account. If so, maybe the purpose of that savings account is to have enough money for that special Hawaiian vacation. For the sake of discussion, let's assume that at this point, you have accumulated a sizable sum. You worked hard to save the cash for that long-desired trip to Hawaii. And while reviewing your options of places to stay, you come across a luxurious, yet affordable, resort with lots of enticing photos and videos to reinforce its status. But if we were to be honest with ourselves, what would really help clinch the deal is customer reviews.

Statistically speaking, what if 10% of all travelers gave the resort less than 5 stars. Would you spend your savings on this resort? What if we rewrite that statement as 90% of all travelers gave the resort 5-stars. Now are you ready to book the trip? I mention this situation because it shows how the framing effect can indirectly impact your ability in terms of spending your money wisely.

> **MY POOR FRIEND**
>
> A good friend of mine once informed me that she had a retirement account balance of $1,000,000 as a result of stashing away $1,000 every month for 20 years. From my rough estimate that's $760,000 derived from $240,000 of cumulative savings. Sounds pretty good! But yet my friend was miserable and was very disappointed with the investment performance. In fact, she kept on telling me how much of a failure she was at saving up for retirement. I was perplexed by this statement and it led to me inquiring about those numbers I just shared.
>
> By the way, I purposely left out one important detail: the year was 2008 and after we witnessed a historical 50% decline in the stock market. Prior to that, my friend's retirement account was climbing to nearly $2 million. So, in her eyes, she was a loser, not a winner.

Let's shift our focus to investing. You've heard the mantra time and time again, "buy low, sell high," Based on your own investment performance, you might see yourself as an above average investor and firmly believe you do a pretty good job of asset allocation. However, those financial decisions are subjected to framing too.

If you ever contemplated the purchase of a particular stock, it's more than likely you have watched its price for a period of time and were considering at what price should you go in? So let's put some numbers to this illustration and say a given stock is currently selling for $110 per share. For comparison, this same security was selling for $100 just a few weeks ago. And, based on what you may have read, watched or even informed by your peers, the company of the underlying stock has consistently made a profit. From a historical perspective, its price has been growing an average of 20% year-over-year for the past three years. Sounds like a fairly healthy stock to consider, does it not? Ready to buy?

But what if I present to you one more additional tidbit of information? What if I told you that this stock has failed to meet analysts' expectations for the past, most recent, three quarters. In fact, the stock price, based on those expectations, is considered overvalued. Are you equally as interested in purchasing shares of this same stock?

If there is one behavioral risk I feel we are heavily exposed to, it is definitely the framing effect. Like many financial behaviors, framing can be a friend or foe. Let's chat about how we can address the impact of this cognitive bias on your ability to manage your money.

## A TALE ABOUT TOM SAWYER

If you are familiar with the famous writings of Mark Twain and the Adventures of Tom Sawyer,[12] you might recall the infamous fence scene from that novel. This is where Tom, as in many of his mischievous activities, gets caught, this time by his Aunt, and instructs him to paint the fence outside the home as a form of punishment. Now Tom, being one who is often able to trick others to get what he wants or to avoid tasks that are not of his desire, desperately does not want to be stuck having to paint this fence. So as his friend Ben comes walking along...Ben begins to ridicule him for his penance.

But Tom, using framing, returns a look of confusion and explains how this is not a punishment, it's unbelievable fun and a pleasure to have this opportunity that does not come often in life. He convinces him that painting the fence is the furthest thing from work. And simply says, "...you don't get to do this everyday" as if it were a once-in-a-lifetime activity, a privilege.

From this perspective, Ben begins to see this no longer as a chore, but a treat and can't help himself but ask, "Say Tom, let

---

[12] Twain, Mark. The Adventures of Tom Sawyer. The American Publishing Company. Originally published December 1876.

> me paint a little". The ruse worked because in this context, Ben not only begs to want to do the painting for him, even pays him an apple for the privilege. Not long thereafter, Tom has over a dozen kids paying him for the opportunity to participate in this "FUN" activity.

**Actionable Step 1:**

*Widen your lens.* What I mean by that is all frames have borders that are limitations of what you are perceiving. When we go back to the introduction and the crime scene, is this not the reason detectives work so hard to hear as many eyewitness perspectives to gain a more accurate picture and gather as many facts as possible?

One of the best things you can do is become more informed. Seek advice and research you have not heard yet. When I am considering a major purchase, I am a research animal and the tough decision is knowing when I've done enough. What gets most people tripped up is focusing on research that confirms their already preconceived notions about the facts of a situation. That's actually called confirmation bias and we'll be touching on that in a future episode. when you look for information that is only an affirmation of your existing beliefs...it's usually a sign that you haven't gone beyond your current frame of vision.

**Actionable Step 2:**

*Why?* Ask yourself this simple question, but you might not get a simple answer. What is the rationale behind your decision? When you put your thought processes into overdrive, it pushes you to carefully consider why you relied on limited information. This creates the potential realization that your decision may be too heavily influenced by the way associated facts were presented to you at the point when a decision is required.

**Actionable Step 3:**

*Seek out more credible advice.* This is really tough, but consider a certified financial advisor, or someone you know with expertise in a particular financial knowledge, leverage online and offline resources that have proven to be reliable. I often like to find resources that have supporting data or studies to support their reasoning. But there's a caveat, you need to periodically re-examine the advice you obtain from these channels because they too may be anchored to rationale that is dated. By the way, We'll discussing more about anchoring in a future episode.

**Actionable Step 4:**

*Get better at logic puzzles.* In Chapter 3, I mentioned I love brain teasers and here is one of the reasons: They help you think out of the box, or in this case, outside the picture frame. Sounds silly? Well let me give you a great example of how getting better at riddles can help you get better at reducing the framing effect.

Let's go back to the supermarket and this time, instead of cookies, we are shopping for chips and dip. There's a sale, and combined, the chips and dip cost $1.10. We also learned that the chips were $1 more than the dip. And if that is the case, then how much was the dip? (This is where the Jeopardy music should be playing in your head.) Would your response be that the dip cost 10 cents? If you did, you are mistaken. If the dip was 10 cents, and the chips were $1 more than the dip, that would make the chips $1.10. But that cannot be because then the sum of the chips and dip together would be $1.20. The correct answer is the dip price is 5 cents. Think about it. The chips cost a dollar MORE. That would mean the cost of those chips were $1.05. Thereby leaving the dip to be at the price of 5 cents, and thereby giving us $1.10 in total. The point: If you train your brain, you can potentially reduce the cognitive biases that it likes to construct.

I think it's time we revisit the introductory teaser to this chapter and the two friends who shared their interpretations of a painting. Was either one inaccurate in their descriptions? Just consider how limiting their scope would have been if they DIDN'T ask one another about their points of views. Discussing experiences is another way of overcoming the framing effect. So the next time you are at a museum, opt in for the audio guide to expand your perspective too.

# Chapter Seven: Navigationally Challenged

## Key behaviors: Experiential, Conformity and Media Response Biases

*Are you planning to take some vacation this year? Perhaps you're plotting your next road trip, outdoor adventure, fun in the sun or some overseas travel. And when it comes to planning, is it based on your travel experiences? Maybe you feel as though you have greater insights than a typical travel agent? Or, are you someone who combs the web for ideas and recommendations? Do you check out multiple online booking sites or is there one particular booking site that you have used before and will use again? Or do you prefer to organize a trip a la carte and will visit destination websites to make specific choices. And if so, are you relying on reviews or your past experiences?*

*As it turns out, your navigational skills in decision-making, particularly your financial ones, are heavily influenced by your circle of influences and your age.*

Up until now, each chapter focused on one particular behavioral risk impacting your ability to manage your money. In this chapter, we will be mentioning several because the behavioral risks for discussion are in some way interconnected or polarizing to one another.

It's actually quite amazing how many of our decisions are based on singular experiences. Here are a few everyday situations where you made choices based on your recall of previous experiences without possibly realizing it.

Have you ever ordered a disappointing plate of Pad Thai from your nearby noodle restaurant? And after such an unpleasant experience, are you going to order from them when you have a craving for pad thai again? Probably not, but what if it was a fluke. What if the regular chef happened to be out sick that day, or maybe since then, new management took over?

Here's another. Consider that your favorite shoe outlet is having an attractive sale, and you've fallen in love with a pair of shoes you found online that are in stock locally. And you think to yourself, "why not get them today." So, you hop in your car, drive to the store, and speak to a salesperson who was just downright nasty. The brick-and-mortar shop had the shoe, but the miserable interaction with the employee left you with a less-than-stellar feeling about the store. I'm betting the next time, you'll order online to avoid that experience again or perhaps you won't buy from them ever again. But what if everyone else working there is pleasant, what if that person quit or got fired not long thereafter, or maybe something awful just happened in their life not long before you stepped foot into the store?

How about engagements you have had with co-workers on the job? Tell me if you have not been in the following situation: For the sake of the example, let's say your co-worker's name is Leslie and the last project you worked on with Leslie was not very amicable to put it lightly. Not long thereafter having this experience, a fellow worker mentions they are to embark on a new project and asks if they should reach out to Leslie for assistance. I would predict your response will be to state how awful Leslie was as a business partner. You express how there was a lack of attention, time and detail needed and, if at all possible, avoid working with that person at all costs. But what if there were factors at that period when you worked with Leslie that prevented the proper attention, time or resources necessary to making your project a priority?

If we hit the rewind button, we could turn around each story into positive inferences too. The Pad Thai, could have been superb because the usual chef was not cooking that night. The salesperson in the shoe store may have complimented you on how good those shoes looked on you and gave you a shoehorn for free with your purchase. And as far as Leslie goes, maybe you achieved great success and an extremely productive collaboration that resulted in measurable results because it was at an opportune time when Leslie was able to dedicate more resources to your needs.

In each of the three examples mentioned, a singular bad experience or a singular positive experience, affected your future decisions when seeking to satisfy a similar need or want. If you were right in front of me at this moment, perhaps you would respond: "But Joel, I don't always make a decision based on a singular experience. I have years of training, expertise and know-how that validate my decisions."

That's true ... and that can contribute to a higher probability of achieving desired outcomes. Core behaviors are reliable, but they are not how all people or the world act all of the time.

Here's a true-to-life scenario. Is there someone in your personal life or career that is known for how well they successfully managed a situation or project. Maybe you witnessed them receiving accolades, receiving a bonus, pay raise or job title change resulting from that achievement. And let's say in another year or two, a similar challenge arises and because of their experience, are asked to spearhead that project too. In fact, that same individual may follow the same process to ensure above average results again! But there is only one thing—what happens if this time around, it doesn't. This could be a result of a change in audience preferences, resources, technologies, new expectations, different measures of success, etc.

> **LEARNING ISN'T A SAID AND DONE ACTIVITY**
>
> Anyone a fan of astronomy? One day I was enjoying lunch with a good friend and we were engaged in an interesting conversation about our solar system. Now, in my youth, I was taught there were nine planets, which included Pluto. And based on literature and resources, it in fact was considered the ninth planet for many years. Today, it is now categorized as a dwarf planet and lost its status as planet number nine because it does not meet the criteria the International Astronomical Union uses to define a full-sized planet.
>
> But here's the thing, in 2016, astronomers believe they may have discovered and are hunting for a tenth planet that is said to be 10 times the mass of Earth. And that is really fascinating to me, but based on our current knowledge why have some supporters labeled it as the tenth planet. Shouldn't it be the new ninth planet? Experiential biases can pop-up in all sorts of unexpected ways in our world.

All these illustrations are to help drill in a particular behavioral risk—and that's **Experiential Bias.** Experiential bias is when we have gained knowledge and experience in a given area, concept or skill and use what we have gained in making future decisions. So as a result, we tend not to do our homework and are less likely to conduct logical analysis and research that such a decision might dictate. This is especially true when we find ourselves making what we perceive is a similar decision we have made before, but meanwhile the data, facts and logic may have changed. And these behaviors are amplified as we age.

Now anyone reading along who is younger, educated, up-to-date with newer technologies and a keen ability to leverage online resources may feel justified in their common beliefs that those old farts don't get it. Because when we are in our earlier stages of our life, we often claim older people are stuck in their ways and that their own, fresher perspective, is more valuable.

Well not so fast you young whippersnappers. Don't start gloating just yet. Because when you are younger, you are more susceptible to **Conformity Bias.** What's that you say, what is conformity bias? That's when you are more likely to make decisions conforming to current social norms, culture and team or relationship dynamics.

The purchase of a smartphone makes for a great example. You really like the brand named "Universe" based on its improved camera, speed and how well it works with other platforms. But all your friends and family brag and use the smartphone brand named "Orange." You did your research, compared the two, and feel very confident the Universe phone is better, but despite all the supporting facts, you end up getting the Orange. The reason you may have chosen the Orange smartphone is because you are satisfying a strong emotional desire for acceptance and creating group harmony, which may outweigh your ability to make a more rational decision.

Let's go back to the office environment again, where you may have witnessed an extreme form of conformity known as *groupthink*. Just reading the word "groupthink" you are probably nodding your head, saying to yourself, "Yeah, tell me about it."

For visualization, imagine you are in a small conference room or virtual chat room with several business partners. Whether the topic is a business strategy, project, concept, or initiative, they matter not for the point of this exercise. Your role and presence is a direct result of your unique skills and experience. It's expected that you will add value by expanding on your thoughts on the given subject matter.

Have you ever been in any such meeting and it's like you are a spectator at a Broadway show and the entire meeting feels scripted and staged? Here's how it goes: Someone proposes an idea, maybe it's even your own manager. Since it is coming from your boss, everyone around the table starts getting excited and giving that idea more kudos and acceptance.

There's just one hitch. Based on your own experiences, you firmly believe there are facets of the idea that possibly warrant discussion and potentially put the brakes on the suggestion, but at this point there is overwhelming agreement in the room to move forward with a plan to implement. At that moment, you wonder whether or not to figuratively raise your hand and be the party pooper. The sad thing is groupthink is an incredibly powerful behavioral force. And despite choosing to speak up or not, this project is barrelling down the road at top speed.

Let's focus on the implications in our financial decision-making. Back in 2008, the Federal Reserve Bank of Chicago studied the average American's decision-making performance on several financial-oriented decisions.[13] They then plotted their finding into two camps: the first, is *experiential capital*, which measures one's level of experience making financial decisions. And the other, *cognitive capital*, which measures one's ability to analyze information that was necessary to support their financial decisions.

This is incredibly important because when we are younger, we tend to depend more on cognitive capital and we are more receptive to analytical information. Although the study does not necessarily suggest it, I would gather that dependence would include social media as well. As we age, we rely more on our long-standing experience and less on analytical information when making decisions.

The results from the study were then plotted on a chart reflecting experiential capital, which tends to be low at

---

[13] The Age of Reason: Financial Decisions Over the Lifecycle. Federal Reserve Bank of Chicago. August 2008.

younger years and increases to a relatively fixed point at an older age. And analytic capital, very high when we are young moving almost in a straight 45-degree angle to the right as we age. Now a third line was added, and it is based on successful task performance across all ages. From this data, we discover the age of peak performance, which is age 53. That's when, on average, we have the right balance between experiential and analytic capital at work.

So many studies focus on Boomers and Millennials and Gen Z, but what generation seems to be in their prime for decision-making? If you know a Gen Xer, or work with one, you might want to ask for their opinions more often and invite them to more of your meetings.

When it comes to financial decisions, the findings of this study have huge implications, especially as we move closer to or are in retirement. Before then, it's all about asset accumulation and building wealth. You may be familiar with the risks associated with growing your savings and investments along the way.

But here's what's scary, right when you need to make decisions on how to generate income in retirement versus building wealth, your decision-making ability may have declined. And analytically speaking, making choices about how to create an income stream in retirement has different rules, different risks, and a different set of facts to come to a solution.

So, at this critical junction of our lives, there is a strong possibility that you will intuitively rely more on your long-standing financial experience that is misaligned to the need. This phenomenon is also associated with another behavioral risk, *anchoring* behavior, which is the tendency to adhere to prior beliefs longer than one should.

Now let's get back to conformity bias for a moment with some supportive research around it. Way back in 1955 and 1956, Solomon Elliot Asch,[14] a psychologist and a pioneer in social psychology, conducted conformity experiments and released the results in two or more papers at the time.

The classic example of the power of conformity goes something like this. Consider two boxes on a page. The first box has one vertical line in it and nothing else. The second box has three vertical lines of various lengths labeled A, B and C. And respondents of the study were to pick which line: A, B or C is identical in length to the first line. From the illustration, line C is glaringly obvious to be the same exact length as in

---

[14] Asch, S.E. (1955). "Opinions and social pressure". Scientific American. 193 (5): 31–35. And Asch, S.E. (1956). "Studies of independence and conformity. A minority of one against a unanimous majority". Psychological Monographs. 70 (9): 1–70. doi:10.1037/h0093718

the first line. And if you were asked, you would in all likelihood pick C.

But here's the rub. When this was conducted with university students, all but the test subjects initially said the answer was line A, not C—visually it was obviously incorrect. Asch, the researcher, found that the student participants conformed to an incorrect majority roughly one-third of the time and three-fourths conformed to this incorrect answer at least once.

I know this sounds hard to believe, but this experiment has been replicated many times in several ways and levels of conformity may have varied, but it still happened. The discrepancies from a statistical standpoint reflect that despite 75% of the participants agreeing to an incorrect response initially, some were able to break the groupthink mentality and thereby reducing the number of incorrect responses 33% of the time. Some psychologists often believe that the fluctuations were more likely based on the focus of the tests and their associated social norms and culture at the time.

Another sad, but real world example, is the disastrous consequences of groupthink that occurred at NASA. I'm talking about the Columbia space shuttle explosion back in 2003. A panel warned that there were safety problems before the launch. But many members of the group ignored relevant information and had a sense of invulnerability due to the number of successes accumulated with space shuttle missions. Unfortunately, all seven crew members perished as a result.

While not likely to be a life-or-death situation, conformity bias can become a tragedy in terms of financial outcomes and your ability to manage your money. People seem to be more comfortable mimicking others, even regarding monetary choices. I'm sure you have heard the term, "keeping up with the Joneses." How often do we get the latest and greatest name brand electronics, cars, clothing, vacations, homes, toys and more as a need to be in line or one up over our peers.

Conformity bias ignores an important factor. Your financial situation is not the same as everyone else's in the group. And conformity can lead to unaffordability in terms of spending money. The size of your loans and the subsequent monthly payments tethered to credit card purchases or on a larger-than-life car or home, can significantly impact your child's education fund, the size of your nest egg, or your ability to weather the unexpected.

Conformity can be detrimental in terms of investing. I cannot think of a more fitting example than the GameStop fiasco of 2021. Who would have thought that an ailing video game retailer would capture the world's attention. For those who know of it, but really don't quite understand what happened, I'll sum it up in a few sentences. Reddit, which is an online community of people with similar interests, had a page dedicated to WallStreet investing. The authors commented on the frustrations they had with large hedge funds making large amounts of profits and their impact on the value of securities with what they believed little regard for the companies the stocks represented. In particular a hedge fund uses short-selling, which occurs when an investor borrows a security and sells it on the open market, planning to buy it back later for less money.

In a move of vindictive behavior and an opportunity to reap some profits of their own, Reddit page wallstreetbets put out a rallying cry for all its followers to buy GameStop stock, which in turn pushed the stock price to astronomical levels and forcing the hedge funds to buy back at a far higher price as opposed to a cheaper price. Unfortunately, many of those who followed the advice of wall street bets were users of the RobinHood app, which means these were mostly average Americans with not all that much purchasing power, placing investments beyond their means. Without getting into all the details, and because of the market fluctuations, RobinHood prevented many from selling out of the purchases at an opportune time. So while there were some winners, many people with far less assets under their belt were hurt.

This is also an example of what is known as *herding* behavior. However, this also is related to **Media Response Bias,** which I would like to briefly mention here because it fits in well. Media response bias is related news and social media's often optimistic view on products, services and the markets that are very attractive for increased views and readership. Many times you may see or read reasons that feel empowering for you to act because "everybody is doing this and you should too."

Let's get back to the behavioral risks in this chapter's discussion: experiential and conformity bias. What's interesting is that the ways to combat experiential bias are the same as the ways to combat conformity bias. And here they are.

**Actionable Step 1:**

*Stay informed.* Follow and subscribe to trustworthy resources. It's important we continuously keep ourselves educated and knowledgeable. Whether it's online or offline resources or a combination, make sure there is contrast in points of view. And equally important, find yourself one or two mentors or certified financial professionals that you can share your concerns and goals with. Having someone to bounce your money management thoughts can widen your eyes to potentially improved outcomes.

**Actionable Step 2:**

*Balance years of experience with modern know-how.* You probably seek a doctor with years of experience, yet it's equally important that this healthcare professional is up-to-date on all the new procedures available. When it comes to your own money management, you probably made decisions based on your existing experiences at the time you agreed to ongoing expenses, loan rates, savings accounts and short term and long term investment strategies. But when was the last time you compared them to today's personal financing and investing choices? New facts, investment options and technologies—added with your years of experience—may present an opportunity to improve your financial well-being.

As a personal example in the work setting, every Monday morning I would avoid the trap of tackling projects solely on my existing expertise. I would take a fresh look at a project and ask myself, if this was my first day at this role, what new technologies, learning lessons and people would I want to reach out to gain new perspectives. This is true with money too. Periodically (minimally annually) review your expenses, loan rates, savings vehicles and investment strategy to ensure they are aligned to your objectives, because sometimes the smallest life events during the year, may have a profound impact on your financial well-being.

**Actionable Step 3:**

*Become an active listener.* Try not to let your mind wonder. Whether it is someone with financial know-how sharing their experience, a webinar, a conference, or a video tutorial. Keep eye-contact, Show signs you are listening using nods and other non-verbal gestures to express how what is heard is agreeable or not agreeable to you...even if there is no one in the room with you. Restate or write down key points. Ask open-ended questions. Personally, I always keep a notes app, a mini digital whiteboard or just pen and paper with me at all times to jot notes.

And if you are a listener of podcasts (such as the *FinWizdom* podcast,) it's fine to listen while doing a routine chore or activity, just try to avoid picking up the phone or tackling a new project while doing so. Either one will change active listening to passive listening and your ability to retain what you've learned.

**Actionable Step 4:**
*Learn humility.* Hate to break it to you, but for all those who think they have a solid savings, investing or money management strategy, you are not the only person in the world with life experiences. Likewise for those who think they have more financial acumen because you completed a certificate, attended a conference or webinar, read several articles and opinions on social media, or watched a how-to video, that does not equate to hands-on experience. You may be positionally higher in terms of what you have learned about a particular financially-related topic, but everyone has ideas that matter. You can learn from everyone. Mostly you can

learn what to do, but you can also learn what not to do when it comes to money management.

On the flip side, don't confuse humility with passiveness. It's okay to show your strengths and limits. Just remember others are gifted too and it may be an opportunity to help them grow as well.

Although we've gone to great lengths to point out these polarized behavioral risks, there is one common theme to combat them—and that's AWARENESS of the impact of your behavior. Increasing your ability to recognize them can ultimately help you to potentially reduce their influences. And that's why I hope you revisit this book often and continue improving your financial wisdom by listening to FinWizdom. It's a great way to stay alert to the behaviors that impact your financial decision-making.

And so going back to the opening teaser about vacation plans and plotting your course for the ideal trip, I think you realize by now that there is no right answer, because you are going to trust either your experiences or conduct extensive research. But all I can say is: *You don't know, what you don't know.* So if you have travel experience, pretend as if you don't and explore new travel opportunities. If you are the king or queen of bargain travel online, don't rely on the info and reviews only, reach out to someone personally who has visited your desired destination. Either way, expanding your world could lead to the best vacation you ever had.

# Chapter Eight: I've Changed My Mind
## Key behavior: Choice Paralysis

When it comes to summertime, it makes me think of the outdoor green markets. I really enjoy the local offerings of fresh fruits, vegetables, baked goods and so much more. And like me, I bet you specifically look forward to particular vendors or products that you might find there.

One of my favorite tables at the market is this one seller of jams and only a few years ago offered just three basic flavors: strawberry, blueberry and raspberry. I gravitate toward the strawberry jam, but they are all delicious. And every year they would add a new flavor. So, this year, when the green market opened, low and behold they now offered 16 flavors of which included the likes of grape and rhubarb, apricot and maple, apple walnut, mixed berry, blackberry peach, lemon marmalade, plum orange, and other exciting flavors. To help you make a choice, they provide free tastings and I must have tasted almost all of them—and I can tell you I was delighted by every one of them. But here's the strangest thing, I ended up walking away without buying a single jar!

One of the advantages of living in a democracy and the many freedoms we are awarded is the freedom of choice, which extends to the products and services available to us. Just think how many places you can go food shopping in a 10-mile radius from your own home! Or the number of hair salons? Or places to buy a cup of coffee? Or someone to fix your plumbing?

And what about the mind-numbing choices we have at our fingertips? Start on an exploration for a new garment, electronic gizmo, or kitchen gadget and 10 minutes online can easily become 10 hours over the course of a few days between narrowing down options, reading reviews, reading expert advice, seeking peer advice, and then the almighty hunt for the bargain price.

Having choices is a blessing and a curse all at the same time. As an example, I tend to make my own tomato sauce these days, but to save time, I always like to have a premade jar in the cupboard in a pinch. Yet, have you walked down the aisle at the grocery store for tomato sauce? Reading all the labels, there's spaghetti sauce, traditional sauce, marinara, onions and peppers, vegetable, garlic and basil, chunky tomato, roasted tomato, meat-lovers, organic, vegan—the list is endless and that's all just the varieties under one brand. Now multiply brand options by a dozen or so other labels and then you realize why half the aisle in the grocery store or more than one page to order online is dedicated just to tomato sauce.

## DINNER AT THE DINER

Cooking a meal at home after a long week seems like a hassle, so maybe this weekend you want to just head over to the diner for breakfast. What we love about the diner is you can have any course you want any time of day. In theory, this sounds great, but what happens when we start perusing the menu? Well, for starters, are we looking at breakfast, lunch or dinner? How do you want your eggs? Scrambled, boiled, over easy, over hard, fried, just the egg-whites?

Do you want home fries, french fries, hash browns, grits, or bacon, what do you want inside your eggs, onions, peppers, sausage, ham, spinach, mushrooms. Or maybe you are in the mood for pancakes. Want blueberry, strawberry, chocolate, old fashioned?

Perhaps I want french toast as a substitute, or maybe just some plain old toast. Again, more choices. There is rye, whole wheat, country white, raisin, and 7-grain. Once again, other choices come to mind such as a pastry, a croissant, or a cinnamon roll. It's getting complicated. Maybe I should select Diner Dan's special #5 that combines scrambled eggs, with a short stack of pancakes and your choice of sides. Wow, so glad we got away from the hassle of making breakfast at home this morning! (Said with sarcasm.)

We experience this difficulty with choices with major purchases too. Many working Americans now have a hybrid employment environment and working from home lends itself to the need for a better laptop. I'm curious: have you gone shopping for one lately? First you need to think of how that laptop will be used and the speed you need, the types of WiFi bands, the size of your screen, the amount of running memory, the amount of storage memory, the software platforms, the types of chips, whether it's a touchscreen, cloud-based, tablet, the plug-ins and the keyboard. Did we talk about colors yet?

How about shopping for a new car? What size engine, do you prefer cloth or leather seats, the fuel efficiencies, sunroofs, roof racks, cargo space, digital dashboard options, and the like. Oh, and I neglected to begin with which model and make and year. Should we talk about colors again?

Have you ever shopped for a new home in one of those communities that they customize to your personal tastes? Want one or two garages, want a pool, how many rooms do you want? Do you want a second floor and/or an attic? What kind of window treatments? Would you like the granite counters in the kitchen, as well as molding on the top and bottom of your floors? It just doesn't seem to end.

You don't even need to be face-to-face with a salesperson or physically present. Just the other day, I was shopping for some upscale flip flops from a well-known online retailer. I even knew the brand I wanted and acknowledged the pair I desired would cost a tad more. I thought the hard decisions were already made and thought to myself, "this should be easy enough, just pick a color and click the button." But then I noticed different reviews about different sellers and feedback regarding the quality of construction. Okay, great. I got over that hurdle, but now I have to choose from not 5, not 10, not 15, but from 26—I am not joking—26 different colors.

I have to stop here because the examples are exhausting and my mind is racing with so many scenarios where the appeal of freedom of choice can actually become quite restraining. And this feeling of overload is called **Choice Paralysis.**

When it comes to managing your money, there is a world of information, tools and advice at your disposal that are there to help you make sound decisions about your finances. Yet despite all these resources, and the intent to help you select the appropriate solution aligned to your goals and objectives, choice paralysis can trip you up. Unfortunately, all that information may not be organized in a way that is easy to analyze or applicable to your specific financial needs. Overwhelming good intentions to either help you efficiently borrow money or to make sound investments can leave you more confused than where you started.

Even people with higher levels of financial acumen can get tripped up by loan options. In a few chapters, I have cited mortgages for one reason or another. The reason for the continual focus is because in all likelihood, a home may be the largest purchase and loan commitment you may ever have in your life.

The decisions you make in terms of lending options can have a significant impact on your wallet, especially when we are talking about loans that take 15 to 30 or more years to pay off. And when it comes to choice paralysis, mortgages are right in there. Forget about the exhausting efforts to find your perfect abode, financing options can be overwhelming. When it comes to mortgages, you need to consider a number of types that include conventional, fixed rate, adjustable rate, jumbo, government-backed, 10- to 40-year terms, no points, with points, preferred rates and waived closing costs.

As of June 2021, there are approximately 4,430 commercial banks, 640 savings institutions, and 5,160 credit unions in the United States waiting to lend you money. Now you won't find it too difficult to obtain information on any of these mortgage options, but you definitely are challenged by the number of choices.

### ZERO FINANCING AT THE AUTO DEALERSHIP

Choice paralysis with regard to the process of purchasing a car makes me want to share a little logic puzzle when it comes to financing a vehicle. If you recall in Chapter 6, we discussed the influences of how these choices are framed may influence our financial decision-making.

In my younger years, car dealerships used to offer zero financing if you paid the car off in 2 years. The offers fluctuated as some dealerships promoted up to 5 years to pay off a loan with zero down at zero percent...wow...what could be wrong with that! Well, it turns out you could be losing money if you don't take out an auto loan with interest. I bet you are tilting your head with that statement. So please permit me to explain.

Let's say you are in the market for a vehicle that retails for $30,000 and the dealer offers you that 5 years, zero down at zero percent interest just mentioned. That would equate to monthly payments of $500 over the course of 60 months. However, what if the dealer offers you a choice in the way of a cash back rebate, say $3,500, if you pay in full for the car instead?

At the same time, let us assume you can find financing through a bank or credit union at a rate of 4%. Zero percent from the dealer sounds better right? But bear with me, because things are going to start to sound a little wonky.

If you took financing with the bank, you could use that loan to pay the full price of that car and receive that $3,500 cash back incentive. And let's say you had $3,500 in your savings to use toward the car purchase and applied the cash back to replenish your savings upon receipt. This would reduce the

> borrowed amount from $30,000 to $26,500. Effectively reducing your monthly payments to about $488, that's $12 a month less than zero down. At the end of 60 months that is a savings of $720 despite paying interest to the bank for the loan. Now I know that it isn't a huge savings and, depending on the cash rebate and the value of the car, this may not come out in your favor, but the point is that despite having all the information about your choices, you still may not make an optimal choice.

Let's talk about the science of choices. Richard Thaler, who is considered a foundational leader in behavioral economics along with Cass Sunstein, another well-known influencer in the field, are often cited for their work and research that defined what is known as *choice architecture*. It's outlined in the book they authored back in 2008, entitled Nudge.[15] So what is choice architecture? Let's use an analogy to help explain it.

In the digital world, including social media, building a website or an app, mapping a customer journey and conducting user testing helps to analyze and recognize the path one may take subject to the way information is presented. The intent is to organize, structure, and label content in a way that supports

---

[15] Thaler, Richard H. and Sunstein, Cass R. Nudge: Improving Decisions about Health, Wealth, and Happiness. Yale University Press. April 2008.

usability and findability to improve engagement, and in the end, provide a desirable experience and outcomes for users. This science is called *information architecture*.

Choice architecture, the term coined by Thaler and Sunstein, refers to how CHOICES are organized, structured and labeled in a way that can potentially influence your decision-making. The intent is to help "nudge" you, as in the title of the book associated with this science, in an effort to potentially improve your judgments. Often a nudge is associated by establishing an anchor, a point of reference for your decision-making.

For example, we mentioned shopping for both homes and cars earlier. I'm assuming if you were in the market for either one that you had an established dollar value you were willing to pay for your new home or new car. I'm curious. Did you happen to search online and utilize a financial calculator to determine how much home or how much car could you afford? And did you happen to tinker with numbers to see the impact of putting more of a down payment or the change in interest rate or the number of years to pay off that loan would impact your affordability?

Using those calculators establishes an anchor to a specific price and a nudge for you to perhaps save more, find a lower interest rate or potentially influence the length of the loan. This is also an extremely prevalent behavior in the planning for college or retirement. Two really big financial commitments.

Another example where we have all witnessed the use of nudges is with charity fund-raisers you receive in your mailbox or inbox all the time. When asking for contributions have you noticed the choice of donation levels with a box to check off your selected amount? Are you going to donate $10, $25, $50, $100 or enter in your amount? Maybe the charitable request is for a really good cause, but at this point you are limiting your donation to the smallest choice, so you check the box for $10 and provide the corresponding payment information.

Here's where it gets interesting. Change the anchoring scale (the choices of donation levels) and remove the $10 option. There's a strong probability if you are seeking to donate the minimum, you will not hesitate sending in $25 because that is the suggested starting point.

Here's another nudge you may have seen with similar charity fund-raisers. Let's say we go back to the first example with suggested donation options ranging from $10 to $100. However, this time a circle surrounds the $50 option with a caption that reads, "donate at this level and receive a free tote bag set (or travel mug, or blanket, etc.)." This will nudge, or incentivize, you to select the higher, recommended amount.

It is impossible to talk about decision-making and nudges without discussing social influences. Social influences are one the most powerful ways to make a nudge (good or bad). That's because as human beings we learn most from each other. It's how individuals, and societies, develop. The challenge with social influences, such as social media, is they can also spawn misconceptions and widespread biases, which can hurt rather than help. Have you ever made a stock purchase because of all the hype you've read or heard from investment experts in your circle of trust? I know I have and I can tell you that they were definitely not all winners for me in hindsight.

Can you think of a few other financial decisions in your life where you were sitting on the fence and were influenced by social media, blogs, reviews, or general conversations pertaining to the subject matter at hand? We can illustrate this point if you ever considered buying the latest version of a smartphone. This is an honesty test: Were you in the market for one because you actually needed a replacement, or was all the conversation and hype about the latest and greatest wooing you to make the purchase? And let's say you initially exerted the will-power to avoid caving into peer pressure and all the publicity, but then you were bombarded by the promotional nudges. Those discounts, special add-on features or trade-in discounts are there to make it easier for you to take action.

When it comes to financial planning, a nudge can be as simple as a statement with steps you can take to accomplish a recommendation. As an example, receiving advice to establish an emergency fund for the unexpected along with implied actions such as a dollar amount to save per paycheck until you have six months' security saved up. While we are in the discussion of financial planning, it is nearly impossible to avoid the mantra "save more for retirement." However, that phrase means something different to everyone and the key to achieving that goal is establishing the most appropriate nudges from a reliable source.

Keep in mind, nudges don't remove or limit your options, they simply entice you to make certain decisions. This brings me back to the teaser intro of this chapter and why, with all the nudges to buy a variety of jams, caused me to have choice paralysis. An incorrect assumption by many businesses is to assume that the more choices offered in terms of products and services will increase the likelihood customers will be able to find just the right thing. The intent of the seller of jams at the green market, I am sure, was to give me a free taste to influence a purchase. Oddly enough, there is actually research that was conducted with jams that mirrors my personal experience.

A little over two decades ago, psychologists Sheena Iyengar and Mark Lepper published their findings[16] of an intriguing

---

[16] Iyengar, S. S., & Lepper, M. R. (2000). When choice is demotivating: Can one desire too much of a good thing? Journal of Personality and Social Psychology, 79(6), (pp. 995–1006).

experiment to test the impact of choices on our psyche. Here's what they did: They set up a table inside an upscale grocery store. And on that table, shoppers were exposed to a display consisting of 24 varieties of gourmet jam. Shoppers who visited the display were able to sample all the flavors. (Is this sounding familiar?) For the record, those who had a taste, also received a coupon for $1 off any jam. They recorded the number of shoppers who stopped by the table and took a taste as well as how many of those shoppers made an actual purchase.

On a different day, they set up a table once again. Only this time, the number of jams to choose from was reduced from 24 to just 6. Again, making note who sampled the jams and who made a purchase.

Here's what they discovered. Although the larger display of varieties attracted more interest than the small one, in other words more awareness and traffic, when it came to purchases, people who were exposed to 24 varieties were one-tenth as likely to buy as people who saw only 6 varieties!

Logically, we think the more choices people have, the better off they are, but that is just not the case. I'm not saying choice is a bad thing...it's a good thing. However, there is a diminishing marginal utility as you add more options. By the way, diminishing marginal utility is just a fancy way to say that the addition of more alternatives reduces the overall value of the offering. Think of it this way. It's raining and you need an umbrella. You definitely need one, but once you find one that satisfies the need, the more umbrellas with additional functionality subtracts a little less to the overall benefit you would receive from a choice that simply will keep you dry.

So when it comes to financial decision making, how can you make choice architecture work for you? Well, you may not realize it, but it's EVERYWHERE! Many financial institutions and financial resources implement choice architecture to one degree or another. Nudges come in the form of the number of choices, decision aids such as financial calculators, defaults and additional selections based on time or triggers.

Let's start with nudges in terms of limiting the number of choices. A good example of this are credit cards. There must be dozens of card variations out there, but we often associate specific financial firms or brands with particular benefits—and that's intentional. Each organization can offer anything, but not everything. Otherwise, as we discussed, no one will buy. So the nudge is providing an array of credit cards with specific benefits that resonate with particular target audiences.

*Decision aids* are a form of choice architecture that incentivize you to take action. If we stick with our example of credit cards, a decision aid could be anything from free balance transfers, fixed initial rate, additional points when you sign up, travel rewards, premium services, etc. Decision aids could also be in the form of financial calculators.

I've mentioned earlier about online calculators for how much car or house you can afford, but if you ever opened an investment account you may have completed what is referred to as a risk-tolerance questionnaire. You may not know it by name, but it is a set of questions that are often asked to help determine how comfortable you are with risk. This decision aid nudges you toward investments that are aligned to how conservative versus how aggressive you are about investment performance.

The next is *defaults*. This is a big one and has been studied heavily over the past 10 years. Defaults, when correctly established, are there to help us make decisions that benefit us, but again, do not eliminate the choices. In essence, defaults encourage you toward a desired action or activity, and only if you take an alternative, conscious step on your own will a different result occur.

Think of your place of employment. You are often encouraged to save for retirement through a 401(k) or similar program. The nudge in these instances is your employer matching a certain percentage of what you put in. Another more assertive use of this scenario is when a minimum amount per paycheck goes into your retirement plan, unless YOU check off the box stating you don't want to invest. This "automatic enrollment" approach has been very successful in helping people save more in their retirement plans.

The last useful tool in choice architecture is *triggering* additional selections at the appropriate time. I'm going to go back to the risk tolerance questionnaire mentioned a few minutes ago. So let's say you completed a few questions, and based on your responses, you are what is considered a moderate investor. Another question you may be asked is your age or the age you want to retire. A third, if we're looking at truly comprehensive financial planning, may ask questions to help determine your behavioral style. Once those additional factors are known, you may receive a set of specific investments to consider. These selections are nudges to help improve the alignment of your investments with your level of risk, behavioral style and purpose.

Now, that is what financial servicing organizations may be doing for you, but you might be asking, "what can I do to make choice architecture work for me?" An objective of nudges is to build more confidence that the decisions you make are more fulfilling.

**Actionable Step 1:**
*Anything you can do to reduce the number of selections can help reduce decision fatigue.* You probably do a fairly good job of research before you make financial decisions, whether

that's borrowing, saving, spending or investing, but also use lists to streamline choices.

**Actionable Step 2:**

*Create a decision process.* That list just mentioned, add a column to the left and to the right of that list. On the right, add the number one reason this choice is differentiated or unique to all others. Use the column to the left for ranking purposes when your list is complete. I often use an app on my phone that allows me to make simple notes and move around the order thereafter.

Establish a disqualifier criteria, such as what characteristics of a choice will NOT be acceptable regardless of its benefits?

**Actionable Step 3:**

*Review choices during the time of day when you are most alert and have historically made the best decisions.* Studies have shown the morning time has been the best for most people, but I have met many people who run on a different decision clock.

**Actionable Step 4:**

*Create a deadline.* Have a decision plan with a due date. Now I realize some decisions you encounter need to be made in that moment and not in a day or week or month, but when there is an overwhelming number of choices, you can set a limit to how many options you are willing to consider and stop once you reach that point.

**Actionable Step 5:**

*Stop second-guessing yourself and get help when you feel overwhelmed.* I don't mean start reading more reviews online or articles on the subject matter. I mean get someone to weigh in who is knowledgeable, or that is impacted by your final decision. I have one caveat with this. Those individuals should be provided with your decision list so they have full information of your rationale.

And so the next time you are deciding among flavors of jam, but get into a jam over deciding which one you like most, I ask the seller to surprise me and turn the decision over to them (especially when any choice is a good option).

## Chapter Nine: Anchors Away
### Key behavior: Anchoring Effect

*On a fine sunny day, a ship was in the harbor. All of a sudden the ship began to sink. There was no storm and nothing wrong with the ship yet it sank right in front of the spectators eyes. What caused the ship to sink?*

There are two answers to this riddle. One is the response intended by its authors and the second, is far more applicable to your own psyche. We're going to explore what can potentially sink your ship when it comes to your financial-decision making.

I've lived in Manhattan for well-over two decades. And during my travels, you come across many people who have visited New York City at one time or another for business, for family or for fun. What's intriguing is the diverse descriptions of their experiences each person had while there. And I am sure that when asked, "what one should do when planning a visit to the Big Apple?", you are going to receive widely different responses.

They may mention some must-see exhibits, like recognizable artwork at the M.C. Escher Experience in Brooklyn or the Broadway production of Guys and Dolls, maybe it's a famous restaurant like the 2nd Avenue Deli, or going shopping at Century 21 near Ground Zero or perhaps you're a lover of Latin Music and talk up the Copacabana Club in Hell's kitchen. So, I have to ask: Do any or all of these mentionables sound familiar to you too?

Well guess what. If you took up your friend's advice to see any of these places, all I can tell you is that you will be spending more time walking the streets of New York than you would have ever planned and quite disappointed. That's because every single one of these venues have moved locations or is now closed.

The M.C. Escher Experience—that was a temporary exhibit for less than a year that closed back in early 2019. Guys and Dolls—I saw a production back in the 90s and another around 2010, but you aren't going to find it on Broadway at this very moment. The 2nd Avenue Deli? They aren't even on 2nd avenue anymore—they're on 3rd avenue and 33rd St. And as far as the shopping sprees at Century 21 or grooving to the Latin tunes at the Copacabana—they are both victims of the economic cost of COVID-19 pandemic and no longer open for business.

My point is your advice-giving and decision-making are impacted by what is called the **Anchoring Effect**. This is our tendency to rely heavily on our personal experiences or static information, which in turn can distort our ability to derive optimal solutions. In fact, some of those decisions are not merely distorted, they can take us down a path that is completely in the opposite direction.

Let's take a different perspective. Maybe you are someone who prefers to do your own research and you're simply on the hunt for a great place to dine. So, you explore the web, looking for the top 10 restaurants in a given city—and there they pop up on your screen. That was easy, right? Now you start reading the reviews, narrow your choices and make reservations. Well, please excuse the eye-opening revelation, but you just went through several levels of anchoring without even knowing it.

Shall we go through them?

For starters, how do you know the source of this ranking isn't paid to promote those top ten restaurants or even aware of the criteria used to score them, or are they the opinions of the author alone? Regardless, now those top 10 restaurants have been planted in your brain and you will compare all others to them. That's anchor #1.

You invested time in reading the reviews and as a result, you will now set your expectations for each restaurant on those opinions. The food will also need to live up to those opinions. That's anchor #2.

Another issue: Those reviews are based on OTHER people's experiences based on OTHER people's anchoring biases. What do I mean by that? Let's say someone raves about a restaurant as the best dining experience ever. What are they basing their opinions on? Do they have the same taste buds or passion for certain types of food as you do? Would you value the opinion less, if you learned the reviewer mostly ate fast food? So just about any true sit-down restaurant is a fancy feast in their eyes. That's anchor #3.

And here's something to blow your mind: Just the fact of seeking information online to learn what others think are the best places to chow down, or to help you make a decision about any interest you may have, is going to establish an anchor.

The sad truth is that anchoring is almost unavoidable. In fact, it is a key component of heuristics. Does that term sound familiar to you? We discussed it in the very first chapter entitled *Temper Tantrums*. As a reminder, heuristics are the necessary shortcuts we use in our mind to help us make choices. They come in the form of our own experiences, the influences we gain from others, and the relevant facts and opinions we discover on our own. All of which equate to leveraging emotions and all of which can potentially become anchors.

A study of this cognitive bias[17] was conducted by Daniel Kahneman and Amos Tversky, If the names sound familiar it's because they were also mentioned in the first chapter and discussed their groundbreaking work on loss aversion. In this study of cognitive bias, a group of participants were asked to estimate the answer to a multiplication problem, and I would like you to try and solve it too. You have 10 seconds. See the first equation below:

**8 x 7 x 6 x 5 x 4 x 3 x 2 x 1**

Have a guestimate? I can tell you that the median response turned out to be 512. Was your answer around there? So now for the second part of the experiment. They transposed the sequence as you see below:

**1 x 2 x 3 x 4 x 5 x 6 x 7 x 8**

When they asked participants in the study to solve for the second equation, the median response interestingly increased to 2,250. (The correct answer by the way is 40,320.)

I'm not trying to test your math skills. The point is we will anchor to the first numbers in a sequence and our resulting responses will be higher. This pattern of responses has been proven in a variety of forms. For example, I can show the

---

[17] Kahneman, Daniel and Tversky, Amos. Judgment under Uncertainty: Heuristics and Biases. Science, Vol. 185. September 1974. (pp. 1124-1131).

outcome of rolling a pair of dice three times and each outcome was 6 or less. Chances are you will increase your assumption that the fourth roll will be less than 6. If the outcome was more than 6, you would have the opposite assumption.

In a different study[18] conducted by Dan Ariely, I have also mentioned his name before. He is a well-respected behaviorist whose work is often cited in the field of behavioral economics. In a particular study, he investigated the power of relativity by asking participants to choose between three choices of houses for sale.

Envision the first choice: a contemporary home, the second: a colonial home with a good roof and a third choice: colonial home with a bad roof. Those asked to select from the three options were more likely to pick the colonial home with a good roof. That's because we not only tend to compare things with one another, but also tend to focus on comparing things that are easily comparable—and avoid comparing things that have larger contrasts. I would argue it also enables us to create a shortcut to faster decision-making and it is embedded in the choices we make when it comes to managing our money.

How about making this a little more personal. Let's say you're in the mood for a simple bowl of your favorite brand of

---

[18] Ariely, Dan. Predictably Irrational: The Hidden Forces That Shape Our Decisions. HarperCollins. February 2008.

cornflakes and you realize that you are out of both milk and cereal. The hunt in the cupboards and fridge also reveals you are running low on all sorts of staple foods in the home. And your significant other, roommate or family member says, "Fear not, I'll go grocery shopping a little later in the day." Now isn't that great. One less thing to worry about.

So that night, this incredibly supportive person comes home with bags of groceries and in fact, they are gloating. They proceed to rant about how they stayed within budget and saved $25 by selecting sale items! They feel like a hero to you for running the time-consuming errand and the successful use of money.

However, as you unload items out of the bag, you see veggies, proteins, cheeses, chips, fruits and the cereal and milk of course—but there's an issue. This isn't your favorite brand of cornflakes and the milk is low-fat, when you prefer nonfat. Now you turn to this person with a sense of confusion, maybe disappointment or frustration and say, "What the heck is this? Why didn't you buy me my cereal and milk?" And they looked back confused and said, "I did! These cornflakes were on sale and the low-fat milk had a longer shelf life...I thought you would be proud of me for my efficient use of our budget."

I'm not going to continue where this goes, because it could get ugly. But this scenario is a result of anchoring. You had set expectations, or should I say, anchoring behavior and were disappointed because it was not what you anticipated to receive. It was efficient use of your budget money, but yet you are left unsatisfied.

And while we are on the concept of saving money when things are on sale, I cannot resist but to hone in on this more. From buying cereal to buying a dress to buying a car, a home, a vacation, or just about anything, we don't feel good if we pay full price do we? It is all about how much we saved! In many cases, this is ludicrous and I'll tell you why. Since we all love taking vacations, how about I use it in an illustration?

Let's say you are interested in taking a trip to Hilton Head, South Carolina for a long weekend. A place known for its Atlantic beaches and golfing. Ideally, you desire to stay in a hotel or bed and breakfast that looks over the water and steps from the shoreline, or one with a complete spa or a combination would be nice too. And after conducting some research, you get the choices down to two places.

One of the choices is a resort right smack on the beach, balconies looking over the ocean, and a popular spa. It's stunning. Definitely an upscale experience. It goes for $800 a night. That's kind of steep. The other is an equally nice resort with two exceptions: It is a block away from the shoreline with a partially obstructed view of the ocean and no spa. However, it costs $300 a night. The plan is to stay in Hilton Head for Friday, Saturday, and Sunday night and leave on Monday. So the cost of the first hotel is $2400 before taxes and fees. The second choice, while not as luxurious, but still quite nice with a free breakfast in the mornings, will cost you $900. Which will you reserve?

Now I am sure some people reading this may find it worthy to spend the extra for all the extras, but I'm guessing the majority of you would keep the $1500 price difference in your wallet and settle on a partially obstructed view. But what if you receive an offer from the luxury hotel on the water with a 25% discount? Wow, you almost never see that and you would be saving $600! Does that change your mind? That is still $1,000 more expensive, but yet you feel good about how much you saved. You might even see it as a once in a lifetime opportunity. That feel good moment is derived from anchoring the value of the luxury hotel at full price and the discounted amount you are willing to pay.

This phenomenon also occurs with many consumer products. You may really love that dress, but there is no way you are going to buy it today unless it is on sale. What about that new smartphone priced over $1,000, and with a manufacturers discount and a trade-in, you'll splurge because of the cost savings yet you would save more if you simply picked a similar model with a little less tech functionality. Here's another example: How about when you get $2000 off the sticker price of a new car—now there's a score. And let's say you were interested in purchasing a new home with an estimated value of $500,000 as stated from an online source and offered $490,000. This psychologically makes you feel you saved

$10,000, but was the estimated value accurate? In each scenario. A starting price point created an anchor.

Nevertheless, I want to go back to our Hilton Head vacation and change the scenario, because anchoring bias can occur in another form. Let's say after narrowing down our selections to two hotels, we now discover a third option. So, the same two options are still available: The luxury hotel by the water line, with a fancy spa and amenities, for $800 a night, or the decent resort with somewhat similar amenities, with no beach front access but free breakfasts for $300 a night. And the new third option is similar to the first, a near carbon-copy experience of the luxury hotel awaits you, but it is about a quarter of the mile up the shoreline. Its price tag however is $200 cheaper at $600 a night.

If I were to take a poll, and if I were to assume what I know about behavior, a great many of you would choose the luxury hotel experience just a little further up the road. This example aligns to the findings of Dan Ariely that we are more likely to make choices between comparative items more similar in nature than different.

Anchoring is one of the most common behavioral risks in managing our money. That's because it is tethered to so many other biases such as loss aversion, recency biases, groupthink, experiential biases, relativity and more. If you think about it, once we manifest a bias, we anchor to experiences and pressures that influence our financial decision-making process.

So here are a few things you can do about it.

**Actionable Step 1:**
*The first step to reducing the anchoring effect is to acknowledge the bias.* The good thing is you are reading about it at this very moment and hopefully from the illustrations shared are able to detect how it occurs! Congratulations because you have taken the first step to reducing the impact of various behaviors on your ability to manage your money.

**Actionable Step 2:**
*Improve your sources of anchors by changing the way you conduct research.* Instead of searching for commonality, seek out as many diverse views about the topic to expand your knowledge. This will also help counteract another effect known as confirmation bias, where you gravitate to finding opinions that confirm your initial belief or anchor about a topic. It's all about increasing your objective resources and determining trusted sources.

**Actionable Step 3:**
*Put a price tag on what you want to buy before you go shopping.* In other words, establish your own anchor. Knowing how much you are willing to pay for an item or service reduces the impact of the sales game. So regardless if that dress or sleek air pods case or beautiful bathroom tiling is on sale, and

if the current price is below the amount you were willing to spend, maybe you should consider the purchase regardless if it is on sale or not. Now you may argue, "what if I hunt for a lower price once I set my limit?" Well then I am going to say that you lied to yourself and have not set the true limit. The point is to set a price. It may be lower than the retail price and therefore it may take a sale to reach your tipping point, but you are not lured by a sale.

**Actionable Step 4:**

*Understand your own behavioral style when it comes to you and your money.* I say this because your anchors are rooted in your emotional connections to setting expectations and levels of satisfaction you will derive from your purchases, savings and investments. Besides, what you define as an optimal choice may be far different in the eyes of others.

And this is the perfect lead-in to revisit the riddle that began this chapter and provide a solution. Let me repeat it to stir up your memory.

On a fine sunny day, a ship was in the harbor. All of a sudden the ship began to sink. There was no storm and nothing wrong with the ship yet it sank right in front of the spectators eyes. What caused the ship to sink?

The traditional answer...is a submarine. But metaphorically, the answer is yourself when you weigh down your financial decision-making with too many anchors.

# Chapter Ten: Your Reward Is Punishment
## Key behavior: Level Noise

*Halloween...a fun holiday we could not wait to partake in as a child. Do you recall the excitement you had in selecting the costume you wanted to wear? I remember all sorts of get-ups I had worn over the years, which include a prisoner, an angel, a mad scientist, the grim reaper, and of course the classic...a ghost. But what was our motivation when we were just kids—but of course, it was the oodles and oodles of bountiful candy we were about to receive simply by trudging around the neighborhood, ringing doorbells and saying that classic phrase, "Trick or Treat."*

*However, despite wearing the same costume and taking the same approach to every door, you were greeted with inconsistent treats. In some cases the size of the chocolate bars varied, maybe it was not even chocolate, maybe it was a roll of candy sweet tarts, or a handful of change because your neighbors ran out of candy and felt guilty, or maybe it was the disappointing popcorn balls Mrs. Hennessey would give out every year.*

In this chapter we're going to discuss how your brain may get tricked into setting incorrect expectations and how the influence of behavioral variability can potentially impact your judgments.

This and the four next chapters that follow will focus on a concept called *behavior variability*, also known as *noise* and its behavioral risk to making judgments. So why don't we start with what noise is and how does it relate to financial decision-making?

Well, for starters, the field of behavioral economics has dedicated a great deal of attention to biases, which is what this book has focused on up to this point. Biases are irrational beliefs or behaviors that can unconsciously influence our decision-making process, but they are behaviors that are consistently observed. In other words, these errors in judgment all follow in the same direction. We can see what type of error each bias has on our decisions. (Like everyone throwing darts and missing the target, but falling on the same area of the dartboard.)

Noise is more closely related to behavioral variability on a very individual level, it's more random. (Picture the darts still missing the target, but they are all over the board.) And this concept has been less studied—until now.

The increased interest in what influences judgment came about from a book entitled Noise. Its authors, who some you heard me name before include Daniel Kahneman, who is considered one of the fathers of behavioral economics, along with award-winning Olivier Sibony and Cass R. Sunstein, has brought to the surface how this behavioral risk has also impacted our ability to make sound judgment. My intent is to go beyond explaining the phenomenon and expressing specifically its impact on financial decision-making.

To understand the differences between biases and noise, here's an example. If we were to learn about a particular product or service that was in the news because of a recall, there may be an entire group of individuals who may form what's called a recency bias because of that information and not purchase that product or service again in the future. But when it's one person within a group who shares a negative experience with a product or service and it influences the decisions made on individuals within the group, that's noise. Both biases and noise are equally contributing and affecting the way you manage your money.

If you are only just scratching the surface of understanding the nuances between the two, that's okay. It's why this chapter and the ones that follow explore these forms of behavioral variability.

Let's crank up the dial and focus on a specific type of noise. Tell me if the following has ever happened to you.

I'm a serious vacation planner. If you are too, I bet you can easily spend hours (if not days and weeks), planning an upcoming vacation with friends or family. For the sake of illustration, let's say in particular, I am planning a trip to Mexico for a 5-day getaway. Cancun to be exact. And just with a few clicks of your keyboard or swipes on your phone, I come to realize there is a wide range of activities to choose from. I know what catches my eye are the ancient ruins and Mayan museums. And realizing these are must-see things to do, I could spend a great deal of time planning to explore the great pyramid of Chichen Itza, the remains of Tulum and the museums with the best exhibits.

So I've mapped out the days while in Cancun to make sure that me and three travel companions do not miss out on any of it! However, when I share this great adventure with my traveling compatriots there seems to be a slight difference in judgment in terms of evaluating activities. Although we are all headed to the same destination and have the same goal, which of course is a relaxing vacation, others in my group had other ideas. One fellow traveler had in mind to just soak in the sun in a hammock on the beach all day with the intent to partake in a few tequila tastings. Another traveler desired to do more outdoor activities such as swimming under the waterfalls, kayaking, ziplining and driving around on an all-terrain vehicle.

What the heck happened? Are we not all going to the same place?

This is **Level Noise**: the behavioral variability of average judgements made by different individuals. It's when we assign different judgments between levels of severity and generosity.

Let's talk about a scenario that relates to noise—literally. Let's say you approach two well-regarded music lovers and critics who are invited to attend a jazz performance. Note it could be any venue, but I have a personal preference for jazz. In any case, the trio on stage play their best and yet, at the end of the set, both critics are somewhat disappointed and will blog about their experiences.

One reviewer takes a softer, empathetic approach, and states that the group has room for improvement, and should take a timeout to practice their musical skills before their next gig. Meanwhile, the other critic lays into the act heavily and writes that the set was awful and listening was unbearable. In the latter review, the critic tells the readers to save their money and look elsewhere for good jazz and advises the jazz group to quit while they are ahead. Wow, talk about assigning different levels of severity to the same experience.

We talked about a scenario where levels of severity deviated between two critics, but this can also occur within the other extreme. The following work situation may be something you, yourself, have experienced.

I am sure that you are a diligent worker and when it comes to an annual performance review, it clearly reflects that you not only met, but exceeded all the goals that were put forth to you. In this current work environment, you may have one boss, but more than one manager you realistically report to, and they all have a say on determining your compensation for a job well done. So let's say all three managers believe you deserve a 5-star rating. However, the rewards differ by manager. One, may believe you deserve a promotion, another believes you deserve a bonus, and the third believes you deserve special projects. This is an example, how level noise can potentially make a reward look like a punishment. And thus, where the title of this chapter was derived.

Earlier I referred to a book entitled, *Noise*, and it mentions several studies in the 70s that were conducted on the judgment of judges and the behavioral variability in criminal case outcomes. What was revealed in the research is unjustified disparities in judgment to individuals convicted of similar crimes. In particular, a study that was published in the Journal of Criminal Law and Criminology during the summer of 1977 supported this finding. In this survey, 47 judges were asked to respond to the same five cases, the same summaries of information such as charges, testimony and previous criminal records of the defendants, and any evidence associated with each case. The results: The recommended sentences varied in range from a whopping 5 years to a mere 30 days. And this was not an isolated incident, when a larger study was conducted in 1981, which involved 208 federal judges to reflect on 16 cases, only 3 of those cases was there unanimous agreement to impose a prison term.*

Think about that for a moment, even those whose role is to judge, experience noise.

So, let's talk about how this type of noise impacts our ability to manage money. Level noise can potentially be the root of the problem when it comes to inequality in loan approvals. You could argue that unconscious bias is present, which are social stereotypes about certain groups of people that individuals form outside their own conscious awareness.

So based on a loan approvers personal judgment (aka the judges of loan cases), you could potentially be declined or approved lending based on social stereotypes, but that is only half the picture. Personal experiences by a loan approver could aggravate what was already an impact of a bias, such as offering a higher loan rate and stricter terms. An example of level noise is where you may have several loan professionals all equally qualified to review the same type of loan application in nature, but each of these loan professionals engage inconsistently in terms of processing times and inconsistent approvals for the same customer.

Let's switch from borrowers to investors. What about your highly prized investment strategy, whether it's a self-directed strategy on an online platform or you've employed an experienced financial planner. In all likelihood, the investment advice you receive may vary from one platform's investment tools to another or from one financial planner to another. I am not saying not to trust the investment advice you receive or that you research, because obtaining expert and experienced advice is always recommended. However, variability in judgment is present despite good intentions.

For example, a financial professional from a bank or accounting firm may have a higher recommendation to reduce expenses, a financial professional from an investment firm may have a higher recommendation to increase your equity portion of your portfolio and a financial professional from a life insurance agency may have a higher recommendation to purchase more protection for your family and your assets. None of these suggested courses of action are necessarily incorrect but the varying expertise from a similar group of individuals we would deem financial professionals can produce level noise.

So what can you do to reduce the noise? Since we began this chapter with a general discussion around noise, the following eight actionable steps combine some general recommendations and those that can specifically help reduce level noise.[19]

## Actionable Step #1:

*Be open-minded.* Recognize that even the best advice and decision-makers may not be in agreement in terms of solutions.

## Actionable Step #2:

*Find a sounding board.* This is someone in your inner circle that is less about giving advice and more about making you question potential biases in a decision. Asking questions that start with "What if..."

## Actionable Step #3:

*Implement decision hygiene.* A good analogy is healthy hygiene like always washing your hands to reduce the possibility of spreading germs. Decision hygiene is when you do your best to scrub potential noise from a decision. One way to do this is to get more than one independent, expert judgment or source about a given situation requiring a decision. The key here is independent. If your sources are unaware how others derive a solution, you are more likely to reduce the impact of noise.

---

[19] Some recommendations are derived directly from the book, Noise authored by Daniel Kahneman, Oliver Sibony and Cass R. Sunstein.

**Actionable Step #4:**

*Focus on accuracy, not individual expression.* This tip is a difficult one to state and actually follow because I am not a believer in addressing how to remove emotions and behavioral variability from decision-making, rather how do you accommodate it. To help reduce individual expression is to seek advice from sources that abide to set rules and regulations to follow. This tip holds especially true for level noise in two ways: First, it holds those who provide recommendations with parameters to reduce variability in forming judgements and second, it may establish and set expectations as to what those possible outcomes may be.

**Actionable Step #5:**

*Think statistically and with an outside view.* Find similarity in past judgements for similar decisions rather than approach each one as a unique challenge—unless it truly is. The average predictions from comparable decision-making help counter noise. This is one of those tips that requires some tiptoeing because you don't want to fall into anchoring biases, which create behavioral risks based on past experiences. However, the culmination of multiple judgements should prevent such a bias as well as help you recognize signs of level noise.

## Actionable Step #6:

*Resist premature intuitions.* These are snap judgments. I think this tip is fairly straightforward. I would just add that initial intuition should not be abandoned, but that a final decision should be formed based on balanced and careful consideration of all that is known about the decision at hand.

## Actionable Step #7:

*Find independent judgements, then aggregate.* This somewhat follows an earlier tip mentioned in the chapter and that's to avoid having those who are to recommend a solution sit in the same room when collaborating on a recommendation. Rather have them first draw their own conclusions independently prior to a meeting, then discuss those conclusions to find the most appropriate judgment. This also is effective in personal decisions: If you have a joint decision to make with your significant other or friends, each of you should jot down your individual recommendations to a situation and then share with one another to further discuss. This helps reduce behavioral variability.

## Actionable Step #8:

*Make judgements scalable.* What this means is to shift away from absolute judgements. This is extremely useful when there are multiple criterias that go into making a decision, which then enables judgements of separate criterias to be ranked and then aggregated. Going back to the example about the employee reporting to various bosses where a reward system is established, scaling the factors that go into that decision and then averaging responses, may lead to a more agreeable judgment.

We'll be conducting deeper dives into other forms of noise in the next few chapters, but before we do, consider this: if you have children who plan on going trick or treating, you might want to instill in them that for each doorbell they ring, not to judge the givers of goodies. That popcorn ball is not a trick, in the eyes of your giving neighbor, it's their belief they are rewarding you with a treat.

# Chapter Eleven: What If I Don't Like You
## Key behavior: Pattern Noise

*It's time once again to take you back to your childhood. Do you remember when you and a group of friends got together to play a game? A game where you had to pick teams. It could have been touch-football, kickball, baseball, ultimate frisbee, dodgeball, a scavenger hunt, team races, or party games like charades, pictionary, you name it—any time you had to pick your teammates. And when it came to selection, did you pick those who were always the most skilled at those games? Or, did you choose based on relationships? I bet you picked your best friends, or an opportunity to forge new friendships, or to deny picking those you didn't like. And even if it was a group of trusted friends where there already was a long-time relationship, you ranked them based on preferences.*

What I just described is a pattern of judgments that creates behavioral variability and it's impacting your financial decision-making. However, before we go directly into how this noise is interfering with your ability to manage money, let's share where this type of disruptor in your judgment occurs in your everyday life.

I'd like to begin this chapter with a story about chocolate. By now I think you realize I happen to have quite the sweet tooth. So chocolate. Specifically, let's get into the dynamics of a box of delectable chocolate truffles in an assortment of flavors. And let's say you were fortunate to receive such a box of treats. Now in this box there are several flavors to choose from. There's the solid dark chocolate truffle, some filled with caramel, others filled with cherry liquor, ones that are hazelnut flavor and finally a row of white chocolate mint.

When I was rattling off the flavors, I am guessing subconsciously, you ranked the order of the truffles based on your previous tasting experiences. My question is, which one will you gravitate toward first, which one comes in second, what about third, fourth and fifth? (If you're like me, that white chocolate doesn't count.) But all kidding aside, the resulting order is probably imprinted on your brain and for the sake of argument, let's say your fave is the hazelnut flavored ones.

Now let's slightly modify the scenario. This time you are presented with a similar box of truffles to be shared amongst a group of friends. And in this box, perhaps some, but not all the same flavors we just discussed are present, and you are offered one to pick. In all likelihood, despite knowing they all come from a top-quality producer of chocolates and the reviews say that each one is an award-winner, you will gravitate to the hazelnut flavored ones.

But what if one of your most trusted friends tells you the white chocolate mint ones are to die for and emphatically says, "You have to try that one!" Would you prioritize which tasty morsel to choose first?

Okay, I'll move away from the sweet tooth references and provide a few other scenarios in your day-to-day life, where there is something toying with your ability to make sound judgments. As an illustration, assume you want to do something for yourself and read a new self-help book this weekend, but which one should you order?

Most likely you value one source over another…repeatedly. It may be your favorite online book seller who is bound to have a "top five" list for you to consider. Maybe a larger influencer comes from recommendations offered by friends and your social media network. Or maybe, you already follow a particular self-help guru like Tony Robbins and choose another book from a line of his titles. Perhaps it's a trusted celebrity endorsement such as a selection from the Oprah Winfrey Book Club. Or, maybe you are like me and research them all and see which books are present in more than one list. (However, that just may simply mean that a publisher of a particular book has a large marketing budget to get the word out everywhere.)

Although each of these channels may be considered a viable source for advice, you are most likely going to prioritize each of these sources in terms of personal experiences.

Speaking of prioritizing, have you ever used a To-Do List? And if so, which one of those items are you going to tackle first? Are you going to address each task you place onto that list based on the ones you feel confident you can accomplish first or the items deemed more challenging? What about those items added to the list that you have never done before? Maybe none of this matters to you, but I am betting it really does.

In both the truffle box and self-help book examples and even when it comes to your to-do list, there is a pattern that occurs. And that's what we're here to discuss: **pattern noise**. Pattern noise is the personal, idiosyncratic responses of judgment to a similar situation that produce a ranking effect. In other words, personal experiences influence judgment and in terms of unequal priority.

An excellent example to drive this home is at work. Think of the last meeting you had where there was a brainstorming session for new ideas or strategy. And for illustration,, say there are three business partners in this meeting. They are all considered experts in the field, but yet you value each of their ideas differently as a result of your individual relationships.

So let's say one contributor is a trusted colleague you have known for five years. The second contributor is the first time they have ever attended a meeting with you. The third contributor is someone who has always discounted your ideas in the past. Whether you intend to or not, those different relationships will impact your acceptance of the ideas that are fostered during that meeting. You are going to rank the value of those ideas based on those relationships.

Someone with a little familiarity to behavioral economics and if you recall a discussion earlier in the book, you could be thinking, "Isn't this associated with an anchoring bias?" And if you are asking, I am glad you did.

Here's the difference: The anchoring effect is our tendency to rely heavily on our personal experiences or static information, which in turn can distort our ability to derive optimal solutions. Another way to describe it is as a phenomenon where an irrelevant reference point, which may have been relevant in the past, influences our decision making simply because it is the first piece of information received or previously known. And think of pattern noise as a dial that can turn up or down the volume on that anchoring bias. Because it too is based on personal experiences, but it takes what we know and unequally rank those experiences.

Interestingly enough, I came across a study about the two, appropriately named "Noise Increases Anchoring Effect"[20] that

---

[20] Lee, Chang-Yuan and Morewedge, Carey K. Noise Increases Anchoring Effects. Psychology Science. Vol. 33, Issue 1. December 8, 2021.

was recently published in Psychology Science. The research was conducted by a PhD candidate and professor at Boston University and it substantiates this notion through various testing scenarios. The stimuli in their research ran the gamut of reservation prices for hotels and pricing for donuts, french fries sizes, dog breeds to an array of observable dots on a graph. Each was measured based on noise magnitude on a given anchor associated with each scenario.

For example, anchors in the minds of the participants were established by first introducing hotel rates as either a price for a 1-star vs 5-star hotel before sharing a range of options. In the french fries test where participants had to guess calories of varying sizes, an anchor was established by first asking participants to guess the number of calories for a kid's size before estimating the calories for larger sizes. The results had shown that in general, noise itself did not produce anchoring effects. However, noise in the form of significantly lower to significantly higher prices in terms of responses in the hotel scenario, and significant variability in the counting of calories in the french fries scenario, amplified anchoring bias as a result of establishing different relationships for each judgment and produced an uneven ranking effect.

When it comes to financial decision making, pattern noise, in all likelihood, disrupts your ability to manage money. Here's my question to you: Where do you obtain financial advice? If there was a significant market correction and you read in a social media group that you should move all your assets into fixed income, would you believe that advice? What if the same advice came from a certified financial planner? What if you read it in a financial publication you subscribe to? What if the recommendation came from a family member or friend? The advice is the same for the same situation, yet you rank and prioritize the advice based on your personal experiences with each source of advice. That's pattern noise. And this illustration could have been as easy about advice to determine whether or not to place money in a specific investment opportunity.

The following example is one of my favorites: We all have a credit card we use preferably over the others in our wallet. What would it take for you to change the credit card you use to make your most frequent purchases? And let's say you have three to choose from and that regardless which one you pull out, they each have a similar incentive.

One gives you 1% cashback and it is the oldest and first credit card you ever received. The second card gives 1% back in travel credits to your favorite airline and the third card gives back 1% with options from cash back, travel credits, or toward special perks, but you have had several negative experiences with the bank's customer service associated with that card. The point I am getting at is not which one you will actually use, but that pattern noise you may not realize you are experiencing. Once again, we are looking at similar circumstances, similar benefits, but you are ranking and prioritizing your credit card usage based on different relationships.

I have one last example, but with a slightly different lens. It's more about money you have unexpectedly received versus the money you already have. Let's say it's your birthday! And you're having a birthday party with friends and neighbors and they pool their money together to buy you a $500 gift card that you can use at one of several restaurants locally.

This is where pattern noise comes into the picture, because your various friends and neighbors are most likely to recommend where you should use that gift card. And you are going to rank those recommendations because those suggestions are based on their personal experiences, not yours. So let's say some favor fast food restaurants, while others prefer fine dining establishments. Will you judge their advice based on those personal preferences?

Here are a few thoughts on how to break the pattern in pattern noise. And tips to disrupt pattern noise are like tips to break a bad habit. However, breaking bad habits is quite challenging and requires constant practice until they become natural reactions. On that note, here are some things you can do:

**Actionable Step #1:**

*Create a new reward.* Ever hear of dopamine? It's that "feel-good" chemical in your brain that transmits signals between neurons that create positive inferences to objects, experience and relationships. In this chapter, I cited numerous examples with various options of outcomes. The key here is to try and think about other possible positive outcomes to a situation you may have not yet thought about. When you engage in a new reward, euphoria kicks in and dopamine is released. This can help short-circuit your current unequal prioritizing of relationships and experiences that impact judgment.

**Actionable Step #2:**

*Know your signals.* This is building awareness. Knowing your triggers can help avoid them. Our natural instinct is to rank influences to our judgment. That's not necessarily a bad thing. It's part of how we create short-cuts to decision making, or heuristics. But try not to discount the advice you hear based solely on past experiences.

**Actionable Step #3:**

*Replace bad associations with good ones.* To reduce pattern noise, change the characteristics of the relationships of the influences of your judgments that create unequal prioritization. For example, let's say you are seeking advice from two different sources online in making an important financial decision. The first resource comes from a blog written by an expert you have watched on YouTube and followed. The other comes from a blog written by an expert that you cannot stand their personality. Rather than rank the value of the advice on their personalities, value them on their individual track records in offering sound advice.

**Actionable Step #4:**

*Define what you hope to achieve.* This somewhat piggybacks off what I just mentioned. Try not to discount or over-inflate the influences to your judgment based on personal experiences, but rather how the advice and influences by social, cognitive, and emotional factors are aligned to the goals you have set.

I hope this inspires some new thoughts and important learning lessons in behavioral variability. Before we continue, let's go back to the teaser at the start of the chapter about the childhood dramas of getting picked on a team. Keep in mind, regardless if it was when you were a kid or in your next team-building exercise at work, try not to take offense if your name does not come up first. It's nothing personal in terms of your skills, it just may be personal influences in judgment of the person making the choices.

# Chapter Twelve: I Know What To Do
## Key behavior: Stable Pattern Noise

*True story: Three identical triplets were separated at birth. Each was placed into very different homes with very different environments in terms of parenting. Growing up, none of them knew about the other's existence. But during their teenage years, a miraculous event occurred and the three were reunited. Studies have shown that identical children tend to have similar behaviors, IQs, but despite having similar genetic factors and similar mental capacities, the temperaments and life decisions for these three identical triplets varied based on the environments in which they grew up.*

I think you might find this chapter quite interesting as we discuss how judgments made by individuals with similar traits or expertise, but dissimilar personal belief systems create behavioral variability and once again impact your financial decision-making.

I'd like to ask if you can join me in the following scenario. I am sure you have a local grocery store, hardware store, book store, specialty shop nearby that you have made frequent purchases.

For illustrative purposes, let's think of a community bakery (because you know I cannot help but to always have a story or two relating to food). Anyway, we'll name this store Betty's Bake Shop. And let's say you and a group of friends get together at your regular coffee cafe meetup or sitting around your home, and one of your friends happens to ask the following question, "Has anyone ever bought a pie from Betty's Bake Shop because I heard they have quite the assortment of pies to choose from." Hearing this, you recall the reviews of this bake shop often mention three flavors in particular as the best-selling items: Apple, blueberry and cherry pies. And as luck would have it, you have been there numerous times and are very familiar with the selection and tried them all.

So, of course, you speak up and make mention of this fact and you know the next question that follows: Someone from the group is going to ask you, "So, what's the best pie to buy?" And your response may be that you have tried the apple, blueberry, and cherry pies, but you always gravitate to the cherry pie because it tastes just like the ones your grandma used to serve during your family's annual Thanksgiving feast.

But one of your other friends says, "Hey, not so fast! I've been to Betty's and tried those three pies too, and the way to go is apple. What you'll love about them is they bake them with honeycrisp apples. They are my favorite.

I think you can predict the next part of the story as another friend gives a shout out and says, "I beg to differ with both of you, I too have tried them all and blueberry is the winner! Something about the way the bakery combines the fruit makes it one of the most unique pies you have ever tasted."

Now this story may not sound so strange on the surface. Afterall, this kind of thing happens all the time—but why? How can three people, all pie lovers, all given the same choices from the same source have such unequal prioritization of their responses?

It's challenging because we cannot pinpoint the exact criteria being measured by each of the claims in this scenario, but we know that the results vary based on personality and experience. One attached the pie flavor to a childhood experience, another to a particular category of ingredient, and another on the uniqueness of taste. Not necessarily a big deal in an isolated incident, but what happens when it influences the judgment of others on a consistent basis?

By the way, this illustration could equally have happened as a digital experience. You could have just as easily asked your friends on a social media platform, or read through reviews from three acknowledged experts in the world of tasty pastries, and still find notable variations in judgments about those pies.

In the last chapter, we discussed the influence and effect of pattern noise on our judgments, which in essence how our personal experiences influence judgment in unequal priority and produces a ranking effect. The examples that you have just read takes pattern noise one step further—what we are discussing this time around is **stable pattern noise**, which is the uniqueness of judgments that influence the temperament, (our personal traits) and the variability in assessments that are made in judgment and from the advice we receive. *Yeah, I know that sounds awfully scientific so let me try to explain this with more clarity.*

Think of it this way, *pattern noise* is the impact of your personal influences on choices that are presented to you and that ranking of those options is YOUR own influence and perceptions, whereas *stable pattern noise* is how behavioral variability and ranking of advice or judgments, whether it is you providing the advice to others or from others providing it to you. So again, pattern noise is your personal ranking of choices based on your past experiences (internalized), stable pattern noise is a subset of that where assessments conveyed (externalized) often impact the intuition of others.

At this point, you may begin to feel even further confused when thinking back to an earlier chapter that discussed anchoring or experiential biases. If this thought came across your mind, I am very glad, because it does ... to a certain degree. Once again, think of noise as a dial that revs up and down this concept of behavioral variability and is more influenced by our individual perceptions than generally acknowledged assumptions.

To help you visualize this concept, I'll use a bookstore as an example. If you were headed to your local bookstore and you were to ask a group of frequent shoppers where you might find the history section, and depending on when each of them last visited the store, will all direct you to the back of the store. However, let's say you arrive at the store, and learn the advice all of them provided was incorrect. The history section was, in fact, recently moved toward the front of the store. That error is based on their past experience, it's a systematic, cognitive error and is an anchoring bias, not behavioral variability. Now, if you were to receive different advice on which history books to read from that section of books, that variability in judgment and advice is derived from stable pattern noise. Got it?

I want to help you detect it when it occurs. So how about an example where you might witness it at work.

How many of you have ever sat in on a meeting for a new product or service, or even brand launch that included various heads of marketing? If you have, then you will definitely be familiar with this scenario:

In this very meeting, one of the topics of discussion is to establish the most effective and impactful marketing campaign to build awareness. There at the table or in your virtual meeting are three well-respected, award-winning marketing directors within your organization who are equally experienced with launching new or improved products or services. However, based on their individual successes and backgrounds, and despite starting with the same benefits of the products, the same target audience, the same goals—each marketing director may prioritize a different set of judgments of what defines a successful launch.

It's at this point you might hear from one or more marketing experts exclaim the same phrase: "I know what to do." (Thus where the title of this chapter was derived.)

The advice you receive may go something like this:

The director from product marketing recommends a focus on features and benefits. The director with ad agency experience recommends promoting the brand. The director representing sales marketing gives convincing arguments it's all about price. These discrepancies, this behavioral variability in judgment, is stable pattern noise in action.

So how does this impact financial decision-making? A few more illustrations should round out this discussion:

If you ever sought to purchase a home, it's more than likely you requested a house assessment to determine if there are any notable, structural issues. In fact, the amount you are willing to pay, or whether or not you continue with the negotiation for that home may depend on it. Let's say you request an additional assessment to obtain a second opinion. During the walkthrough, both assessors discover water damage near a window pane and when you review their separate scorecards, there is a discrepancy in the appraisal in terms of calls-to-action. According to the first assessor's perspective, the windows require replacement. Yet the second assessor reports it to be insignificant, but should continue to be monitored.

If you ever considered an investment and, similar to the example we just did, say you review two separate market analyst reports on the same investment. You are equally likely to witness a disparity in advice based on their situational experiences.

Or maybe you are like me. When I am interested in making a fairly large purchase (such as consumer electronics), I will visit an array of websites to read expert reviews and although they may even recommend the same product model, the reasons to buy vary on different priorities.

Before we get to some words of wisdom from FinWizdom to round out this chapter, I'd like to go back to the opener to this chapter—the story about the triplets separated at birth. As mentioned earlier, it's a true story and there's a documentary on this remarkable story. Its title: *Three Identical Strangers*.[21] I am sure you can locate and stream it online with one of your favorite video platforms. I'd highly recommend it because it is both entertaining and thought-provoking. For more details, the documentary is about three identical siblings, separated at birth through an orphanage as newborns and given to three different adopted families—all with similar dynamics. The one variant observed among the families: different socio-economic levels. These family members were interviewed periodically over 15 years unbeknownst to one another and the core focus of the research was to analyze the classic question: nature vs. nurture.

Amazingly and by accident, the three boys get united in their college years, but as the years go by, there is a dark side to the story. It's a really fascinating journey with many deeper and somewhat disturbing facts I don't have time to discuss, but my perspective and focus here is on how the influences of variant child-rearing (or past experiences) to individuals with similar genetic makeups have the making of stable pattern noise.

Because those individual, situational experiences growing up influenced the temperament to judgment, I believe that noise shaped each boy's attitudes toward life's challenges. There are

---

[21] Three Identical Strangers. Documentary film directed by Tim Wardle, about the lives of Edward Galland, David Kellman, and Robert Shafran. CNN Films; Raw TV. Released January 19, 2018.

an array of studies out there about the behavioral differences between twins separated at birth, but the point of this discussion is how influential stable pattern noise can be to one's decision-making process. Despite all the brothers having similar, mental issues, one was able to cope, one continually see-sawed emotionally, and the third [a sad spoiler alert] took his own life. It's not the happy ending we would hope for.

However, there is hope when it comes to steps to take to combat stable pattern noise:

**Actionable Step #1:**

*Acknowledge that even experts are influenced by past experiences.* Even experts are human. Advice, by definition, is guidance or recommendations offered with regard to prudent future action. But the advice given is based on the success of one's past occurrences. So when you seek help or read reviews or watch videos to ascertain the best route to making a judgment, do all the facts or situations remain the same that impact a decision?

**Actionable Step #2:**

*Know your problem. Know your goal.* Whether it's personal or business, you know this one, but you need to take a different lens to this. Is the advice or input you seek aligned to the same objectives you are attempting to achieve? For example, let's say you are having mobility issues with your arms and your family doctor recommends physical therapy and are given a list of three therapists to choose from. They all have over 5 years' experience, they all have 5-star reviews, but are you going to choose the one who works more closely with legs or the back, or are you going to go to the physical therapist known to work with arms.

When it comes to finances, are you seeking to reduce expenses, achieve a short-term gain or to reach long-term goals? However, one quick note, this is decision making once a problem is defined, if the root of an issue is not discovered yet, the tip is the opposite and you want to make sure you are obtaining different or deviating points of view. Which leads to the next tip.

**Actionable Step #3:**

*Are you the problem?* Have you ever blamed the experts for not achieving an intended result or goal? Did you receive bad advice? Maybe it's not them, it's you. Before making any judgments, are you trying to solve an ongoing challenge or a new one?

Actually, that was a trick question, regardless of the problem, take the view as it is a brand new one and research all the facts today that may impact that decision. There may be new inputs into that equation. Otherwise, you may be influenced by advice for an old problem. And this can be turned around. In order to reduce stable pattern noise, ask those who are part of the decision-making process to take a similar approach. Has any new data, technologies, influences surfaced since the last time judgment had to be made on a similar problem?

**Actionable Step #4:**

*The benefits of machine learning and Artificial Intelligence.* Using artificial intelligence (or AI) has been shown to reduce noise with more common, routine or recurring problems where your intuition alone may not be enough, or perhaps to confirm your intuition. There are many financial tools out there both free and paid, depending on your need and the repercussions of making an incorrect choice about your money. Now, I know AI is a touchy topic and there are rising questions and concerns about using technology in place of human intuition and expertise, but there is a great deal of proof that when used correctly, can help you make more optimal solutions that are best for you. In fact, stay tuned. You're going to read more on this topic in the next chapter.

**Actionable Step #5:**

*Know your behavioral-style.* There are professional companies and tools that can offer a wide range of descriptions to what makes you...you. Just do a search on the web and you'll see what I mean. If you have worked for a fairly large firm, I would guess you have gone through one or more exercises to determine your "color-scheme." (By the way, if you are serious about learning your actual style, look up *DNA Behavior's Natural Behavior Discovery Process*. They offer a self-assessment tool.) You can even start there from what you learned about yourself. Depending on "what makes you tick," influences the types of advice you seek and the judgments you make. It's actually critically important to decision-making and how we align solutions that we deem a good fit.

By now, I hope you are becoming more aware that behavioral risks and the financial decisions you make are impacted by biases, but equally they are impacted by behavioral variability, this noise. Consider again the influences of experiences on those three identical siblings, and we go back to the age-old question of nature versus nurture.

I think we need to look at it as nature AND nurture, rather than an either/or question. Nature always influences our intuition, but if we solely believe it is nature, then we are saying you can never change behavior. I believe nurture can improve upon the decisions we make, it just takes dedication, time and practice to forge new habits.

## Chapter Thirteen: What's The Special Occasion?

### Key behavior: Occasion Noise

*Anyone up for a playful game of rocks, paper, scissors? You know the one, where you and an opponent scream out those three words and release your hand to reveal whether you have forged it into one of those three items. The rules are simple, rock beats scissors, paper beats rock, scissors beats paper. As children, it decides who washes the dishes, who has to try and cross the stream first, who has to retrieve the ball when it lands into the scary Mr. Johnson's backyard. It's an innocent pastime of childhood amusement...or is it? What's fascinating about this innocuous competition, is a presence of an underlying behavioral variability, an adult version of rocks papers scissors, that is a recurring theme in your own judgments.*

It's time to once again take your mind on a little journey. Let's begin with the end of the year, the winter holiday season and family celebrations. Often, we rejoice in the holiday spirit by spending time with family members, whether that's a festive feast hosted by mom and dad, grandparents, your brothers or sisters, cousins and friends. It's your customary gathering at year end and for the most part, you look forward to this event. Every season you have certain expectations: the familiar family members and friends gather at the table, the anticipated bounty of delicious food, heading off to the traditional destination—if you know all of this, why do your expectations differ year-after-year? What changed your feelings, your behavior, and your judgments that modified and varied the experience?

Usually that shift in your mindset was caused by a trigger. It could be involuntary, such as unusual traffic that hindered your arrival and forced dinner to be delayed, or that has altered the level of joy you might expect to receive. It's not that hitting traffic is a complete surprise, but in the past, perhaps it was not normally an issue.

Sometimes that shift in mindset is voluntary. For example, let's say your cousin invites her date to come along and let's also assume you have met this person before and find them less than pleasant. You are already familiar with their personality, in fact, you met at last year's holiday feast. What you recall about their personality is that they are accusatorial, dramatic, self-absorbed, arrogant. (Oh, come on, stop pretending as if you are in the dark. You know the type of person I am describing).

They are the ones where you could proudly mention you walk 10,000 steps a day and they respond by bragging they do 12,000. You share the experience of a recent road trip down the west coast of California and they interject they took a cross country road trip from the east coast to the west. You bring your own recipe for stuffing and everyone comments they love it and...you guessed it...this person has to exclaim that it's good, but they too make a great stuffing and will feel compelled to share all the special ingredients in their version and why theirs is better.

And as a result, you modify your behavior, you make judgments that are inconsistent with similar situations in the past. This holiday season, you are going to take a different tact. My friend, you are experiencing **occasion noise**. This is when all features of a situation or decision remain the same as previous occurrences, yet your judgment differs. Some type of recent exposure or some type of second guessing of expectations alters your decision-making. There seems to be no logical reason for changing your responses, but yet behavioral variability occurs.

Let's shift from a holiday dinner to your financial decision-making. Here are two illustrations to help visualize occasion noise, both at work and in your personal affairs.

At work: Regardless if you are a line worker, salesperson, project manager, product manager, department head, or a C-suite executive, my guess is you have sat in, or have been a contributor to, a budget proposal meeting. For the sake of the illustration, let's say every year you have the same resources to work with (budget dollars, people, technology, etc.). Yet having no change in the head count, the dollars allocated to specific projects or purposes, not even change in target audience, and only incremental development changes to products and services...funds get reallocated every year to eke out greater gains. I'll call this fundamental choice *tinkering with resources based on the occasion*.

Here's an example of what you may expect. Let's say you are an influencer in terms of how that budget for discussion is divided up for use. Prior to the meeting however, you have been reading or listening to information expressing how many of your competitors are increasing money toward research and development. Should you do the same? If you act on that news, that's occasion noise.

What if your firm is publicly acknowledging managers are using a more robust training program or leadership style. Perhaps no one has nudged you to change the way you manage your own team at this point, but exposure to such accolades may influence your judgment in terms of modifying your hiring and training decisions despite all else remaining the same as last year. That's occasion noise.

Here's another example: technology. Now don't get me wrong, technology is definitely one of those categories that heavily influences business decisions. In all likelihood, it is essential to keep an eye on it, but if you already have a budget allocated to it, what spawns the need to even place more money toward it? That's occasion noise.

---

**NOISE IN THE VIRTUAL WORLD**

Even before the pandemic that hit the world in 2020, most of us were already sitting in a great many virtual meetings. Now I recognize every form of technology has its limitations and there's always room for improvement.

However, when the pandemic hit, did your organization experience a change in virtual meeting platforms? I'm sure there were arguments given why the change was deemed a necessity, but did the enhancements truly warrant the time, effort, resources, and training toward a new virtual meeting platform?

I wonder—how many firms witnessed measurable results in production by switching? And by now, your organization may have plans to switch virtual platforms again! In all likelihood, some recent occurrence influenced a decision-maker, which in turn created behavioral variability that led to potentially poor management choices.

Let's switch gears and make this more personal. Have you ever played the lottery? And are you someone who plays specific numbers? Have you ever changed the numbers because of someone's birthday, picked a new number you feel is more lucky? Why? The numbers are always randomly picked? Odds change based on the number of players, but not necessarily on the numbers you pick. This argument could go either way. Why do you let the machine pick your numbers for you rather than just play the same numbers every time? It's not that one way or the other is wrong, it is about consistency in decision-making.

How about a restaurant tip? Let's say you frequent the same restaurant throughout the year. The service is always consistent as is the quality of the food, and you are often greeted by the same server. However, what's the special occasion that encouraged you to increase the tip for the same service you always receive? Was it a birthday celebration or a holiday that prompted you to be more generous today? Yup, occasion noise just happened again.

Going back to the financial world, how about a loan from a bank. As an example, think about if you were offered the same interest rate and terms between two financial institutions and no impact on the total sum you will repay over the life of the loan and the service is equally nice. Would you pick the bank closest to you because it happened to be raining heavily that day? Was the bank lobby nicer? Did the branding or imagery create some form of positive inference to something or someone in your life?

What about choosing among investments? Ever review your retirement investments and despite no life event change, no difference to your planned age for retirement and no change in investment strategy, and witnessing consistent performance, yet you have this urge to to transition those assets into other investments or to another financial institution? Why? What was the occasion that created this inconsistent response? Was it something you read, heard or informed through social media or peers? Maybe someone had shared a particularly bad experience with the same investments or investment firm and despite never witnessing the same experience yourself, your judgment was influenced.

Decades have been spent investigating the psychological influence moods have on our judgment. In particular, I have seen research conducted by Joseph Forgas[22] more recently referenced. He is an Australian social psychologist with many fascinating studies associated with social cognition and a professor at the University of New South Wales. His findings reinforce how one's facial expressions and actions can be

---

[22] Forgas J. P., East R. On being happy and gullible: Mood effects on scepticism and the detection of deception. Journal of Experimental Social Psychology, 44, 1362–1367. 2008.

observed quite differently depending on whether you are in a good mood or bad. But it also influences HOW you think.

And just because you are in a good mood doesn't mean it is always good for decision-making. From one perspective, it may help in terms of improved cooperation, reciprocation and consensus-building, but you may be more likely to accept first impressions as valid without question. While someone in a bad mood may offer more crucial, counter-arguments and challenge quickly accepted solutions.

Ever hear of the footbridge trolley problem? It's an often referred to scenario that questions one's personal moral philosophy. It's a popular dilemma because it involves some moral violation of another person. That's because it relates to your moral decision of whether or not to cause bodily harm to someone else directly and thereby produces a great deal of emotion and careful reasoning. It was originally developed by philosopher Philippa Foot[23] in 1967 and adapted by Judith Jarvis Thomson in 1985, but numerous other philosophers have studied it.

So the scenario: Picture yourself standing upon a footbridge and there on top of the footbridge near you stands a large man who is a stranger and underneath stand five strangers who are about to be killed by a trolley approaching very fast.

---

[23] Foot, Philippa. "The Problem of Abortion and the Doctrine of the Double Effect." Oxford Review 5(1967): 5–15.

And you have to decide, will you push this large man over the footbridge to stop the trolley from killing the five people who are below? It's a tug of war between a utilitarian choice one death to save five and the aversion of the repugnant act to physically push a person to their death. For the record, only a minority of people, roughly 10% surveyed, are actually willing to push the large man to save the other five.

There are variations of this scenario that include a lever, such as the strangers are actually people you know. For example, among the five below stands your brother or sister. The large man is your father and the five below are strangers. All of these obviously tinker with your moral compass.

The reason I mention the footbridge trolly dilemma is twofold. One, in some studies subjects were first exposed to short videos that induced a positive mood before making a decision about the dilemma. Now despite our general sense of morals and ethics, the subjects were three times more willing to push that man off the bridge! Wow.

The point of all this is to drive home the message that moods, a form of occasion noise, can create complex judgment problems and inconsistencies in your decision-making. Now I may not be able to control occasion noise produced by others, but I can provide some tips on how we can reduce its impact or from even being created.

Here are some helpful considerations:

## Actionable Step #1:

*The impact of stress.* Making decisions at peak stress levels can be very detrimental. When emotions are high, your decision-making may vary despite a consistent challenge, problem or situation. For those working from home, ever trying to solve a stressful work-related problem and your partner comes into the room and asks some innocent question that interrupts your thoughts? Only to learn that the ask was something a little less trivial like what do you want to eat for dinner and you say "....honey not now!" The point is to try not to make any judgments when your mood is running high (that goes for both bad moods and good).

## Actionable Step #2:

*Utilize a consistent schedule or process.* Set time on your calendar for specific types of decisions to be made. When you have last eaten, how much sleep, the time of day, when you exercise, etc. all play into generating occasion noise. So if you can make similar decisions on a consistent, recurring basis, make sure to offer responses and judgments around the same time period. A simple example is what intervals of the day are you going to respond to emails? It's also an opportunity to establish tools and processes to define decision outcomes without deliberating over them every time.

**Actionable Step #3:**

*Establishing noiseless rules through the use of Artificial Intelligence (AI) and Machine Learning (ML).* I also mentioned this in an earlier chapter. Just think. What if we could capture more facts, more information that helps improve predictions, spot patterns where even the experts could not always detect, and achieve a better response.

As humans, we are susceptible to our assumptions, stereotypes, biases or mental fatigue. Implementing the use of AI means making decisions based on data and algorithms only. The benefit: The ability to generate results that can be replicated, tested and validated. This implies that ML and AI, if applied properly, have the potential to significantly reduce behavioral variability.

---

CAN WE TRUST ARTIFICIAL INTELLIGENCE?

There's an awful lot of chatter on this topic out there. There are concerns that need to be addressed such as how do we know if it is producing biased outcomes? How do we trust what it is doing or if it is making bad decisions? And how do we know the technology will be misused?

Regardless of the lens you put on it, and the counter-arguments which many are viable, machine learning will be an integral part of the future of financial decision-making and decision-making in general. We also need to be mindful of the

> impact of biases and noise in machine learning, but I think we also need to be cognizant of influences of the programmers themselves. There needs to be testing for noise before the process even begins. The overarching challenge will always be how to make human behavioral variability more predictable.

This takes me back to this chapter's opening teaser: The game Rock-Paper-Scissors, also known as Roshambo. There are theories on how it may be possible to exploit your opponent's predictable patterns, but what is interesting, winners tend to stick with their winning action, while losers tend to switch to the next action in the sequence "Rock-Paper-Scissors". That's very interesting, but there's also a high potential to produce occasion noise. So, my advice to you, children and adults alike: If you feel like you are playing a game of Rock-Paper-Scissors (literally or metaphorically,) I would avoid the temptation to play this type of game for financial decisions and limit its use to merely deciding who washes the dishes tonight.

# Chapter Fourteen: I've Been Bullied By The Group
## Key behavior: Group Amplification

There's a certain point of the day when a particular question comes up. One, that you decided to take the lead on and really want an answer to ... `and at times, requires consensus from an entire group of friends or family, and that question: What's for dinner?

And the discussion may start off on the right foot such as, "I think it is getting late, maybe we should order dinner. Do we want Chinese, Italian, Greek, Mexican, Contemporary American? What is everyone thinking?" And then, someone blurts out, "Hey, remember when we went to the shore and ate those lobster rolls, weren't they the best!" And this is followed by, "O-M-G and what about those spicy grilled cheese sliders you could only get at that one concession stand by the beach!" "Yeah, remember how much fun we had jumping into those waves. Oh, and don't forget those frozen drinks at the tiki bar!" "Hey, and how funny was it when we thought someone took our chairs when we came back from swimming?"

*And it's at this point, you are asking yourself, "Are we ever going to decide on dinner tonight?"*

That intro about dinner could have just as easily been about deciding the toppings that should go on a pizza. But what if it was more complex decision-making such as those associated with vacation planning? We used vacation at Hilton Head earlier, but let's look at the general premise of planning a trip.

There's a reason you would pick a specific vacation destination and my guess is it involves a desired activity that can only be experienced at that location. Something perhaps on your life bucket list. And of course, you want to share this experience with family or friends.

But when you present this vacation opportunity, is someone in the group raining on your parade? Literally bringing up the what if's: "What if it rains? What if it is too crowded? What if we miss our flight connection? I think we ought to stay at this hotel. I think this is too expensive, I think we should do another activity instead. The best place to experience is not at this destination, we should be planning to go elsewhere." I think you get the picture.

The fact of the matter is any one particular adjustment to your instincts and your choices may not seem critical, but when other voices or other judgments begin to outweigh your vision or planning, and influence intended outcomes, the ranking of those priorities tend to change—sometimes in an undesirable direction.

What we are witnessing is the value of judgments going off on a tangent when there is some type of catalyst, some type of intensification occurs where certain voices or groups of voices weigh more heavily in the decision making. And this is called **group amplification**.

And group amplification can happen anywhere, even when you are online. Do you happen to follow any local social group or platform that caters to your community? You know the various forms: Where people may list items for sale, discuss what's new in town, and sadly the occasional shaming of others or organizations.

It may be someone has a bad experience at a local store, an event, a park, or even about specific individuals and uses the given online platform to voice grievances. And despite that their personal experience may be an isolated occurrence—despite not knowing what factors and information pertain to the incident that voice—those perspectives, go askew. The very nature of social media amplifies that voice (that behavioral variability).

You may even submit an innocent post such as "Can anyone recommend a decent plumber?" And what follows is a thread of consciousness that may sound something like this...

"Well whatever you do, don't hire Pete's Plumbing. They were too expensive and I still have a leak." Then the next post comes along and it reads, "Yeah and Pete always drives that dirty van." Which in a possible scenario may be followed by, "and what about that dog he keeps locked up in the van when he services your home. That dog keeps on barking the whole time." Which is of course followed by "why do people treat their dogs that way, whenever I see someone lock their car with a dog inside I contact the animal care services immediately!" And it is at this point, you interject in the thread and say, "So can someone answer my original question: Anyone know a reliable plumber?"

What often occurs in group amplification is this cascading effect and they are extremely pervasive. It can happen in any setting. Small shifts in conversation can produce multiple deviations from the focus of a decision. I also believe that while other forms of behavioral variability can be argued to be more often observed, I believe group amplification can potentially be the most detrimental to judgments.

The concept of group amplification is very observable in your day-to-day lives. A great illustration of this is at work.

Let's say you and five other business partners are establishing a critical business plan. During the meeting, you're discussing the various facets of this plan. And despite the experience and expertise of the professionals at the table, certain voices or groups can potentially weigh more heavily in the decision-making. So if you were setting a timeline for a project, the order and actual steps are swayed by potential amplifiers.

This may be in the form of all sorts of surprising catalysts. An obvious amplifier could be the seniority of the team leader's vision. Another amplifier may be the influence of existing team member relationships and another amplifier could be coffee versus tea lovers ... *wait, what?* Did I just say coffee versus tea lovers? How could my choice of beverage create behavioral variability?

Please permit me to create the scenario within this planning session. Let's say you are a big coffee drinker and everyone knows how much you love the aroma and taste of a decent cup of Joe. Your opinion of the coffee usually served in these conference room meetings is actually quite good. In fact, you kind of look forward to it. It's almost an incentive for you to attend. But this time around, your business partners, who are really into tea, promote that at this meeting you can choose from an assortment of 12 varieties of tea!

This has zero appeal to you. And during the meeting the entire team is sipping away. You witness them having side conversations about the tea experience. And you feel left out and frustrated because you just want the quality coffee that is usually served up. Unintentionally, you may innocently be treated as an outcast during the meeting.

This may seem inconsequential, but it's not! Because the camaraderie among your business partners forged by this indifferent experience can potentially create group amplification and noisy judgment when it comes to this crucial strategic planning. Choices that could have lasting effects on dedicated time, resources and money. It's hard to believe, but the future growth of your business may be influenced by the behavioral variability prompted by teatime.

Group dynamics can potentially generate very different outcomes, and decision ranking—even from minor, or even irrelevant, differences, among members of that group.

But group amplification doesn't know the difference from overactive to underactive. Your internal voice may influence your decision to speak up too. Have you ever been in a classroom, business meeting or social setting and someone influential just shared their supporting evidence why a course of action should be taken and asks the audience, "if anyone disagrees please raise your hand." And all you hear ... is complete silence.

Others may have valid arguments to question the judgment, but the overwhelming hesitation from anyone raising their hand in what may be deemed as defiance amplifies the weight of the voice at the front of the room or leader of a virtual conference call. You might feel intimidated or even bullied into silence (and thus for the title of this chapter). Because group amplification can make you feel like you've been bullied into submission or swayed to go with an overwhelming stream of group consciousness.

Okay so what about your personal ability to manage money? After all these examples, I do not believe it is difficult for you to think of a few instances where amplified noise produced undesirable repercussions to your money situation.

However, I have a great example to share: When it comes to investing, have you ever heard the term "stay the course"? I bet you have. It's sound advice, especially to reach your long-term life goals and to improve your financial wellness. Most of us are not easily swayed if we hear counter-arguments during a one-on-one conversation based on your personal faith, confidence, and personal judgments. But how strong is your willpower when opposing voices become overwhelming to do elsewise?

What if you start reading mainstream media warnings of a huge market dip for various reasons. You see postings on your favorite social media reaffirming the same message and compounding your anxiety as the emotions of investors are on display with grave concerns (the sky is falling). You may even begin to panic as your spouse, family members, friends or your authoritative acquaintances are telling you they already bailed.

Now I am not saying it is or isn't good advice, but what I do know is that more often than not, people miss the highs and lows of entering and exiting a market when it comes to attempting to practice timing and selection in the investment marketplace.

And what about your spending habits? Everyone needs a warm coat to protect from the winter elements, but did you seriously need to spend the money on that famous brand? (I would mention a few by name, but to avoid legal issues, I am not going to nor do I believe I have to.) You know one reference priced as high as $1,000 or more. And how did you come to the conclusion that this was the coat for you? Was it for the same reasons mentioned in terms of investing? Is the coat getting mentioned or promoted in all forms of media? Was it highly socialized? Are friends telling you how they are buying one? That they are the best coats ever?!!

If you have properly set up a budget and have all your expenses accounted for, all your short-term goals and long-term goals covered and have a glorious bucket of money for discretionary expenses, I say go for it if you crave the trendy fashion. Besides, these coats are fantastic on those really cold days. The advertisements and comments brag how these coats will keep you nice and cozy even if you were standing on the Antarctica—how awesome is that.

But according to statistics, New York City, for example, experiences an average of 18 days a year where the weather is below freezing. Do you honestly need this type of coat for most of the winter?

Maybe you live in a place that is somewhat colder or warmer, but at this point, I get a sense that you may want to justify such a purchase and argue a good winter coat can last a lifetime. But the truth is on average people hold a winter coat for no more than five years. And if you took a look at your wardrobe, I bet you buy a new coat more frequently than that. Maybe it's every two winter seasons. And when the weather is that cold, do you even leave your home on those days?

So according to my calculations, you are paying $50 each time for the privilege of wearing that coat. Now you may wear that coat on many, many more days throughout the colder months, but it is more a question of want versus need, and that want probably increased as a result of group amplification.

The point of both these stories is how peer pressure, this group noise, can seriously short-circuit your own reasoning.

## A JURY INFLUENCED

Back in 1954, a well-known film and television writer wrote the teleplay to a remarkable story that moved on to becoming a landmark movie in 1957 that starred some amazing actors for its time that included the likes of Henry Fonda, Lee Cobb, Jack Warden, Jack Klugman...to name a few. Some of these actors are even before my time, but if you happen to look up any of them, you would find they left quite a footprint in Hollywood. And that movie title is *12 Angry Men*.[24]

It's an amazing courtroom drama based on a book by the same name. I often reference and recommend viewing it to those I have given career advice to because of its valuable learning lessons about group dynamics. It's a story about 12 jurors who must decide whether or not they should come to a guilty verdict based on a violent crime that was committed. Now this film examines many facets of influences of diversity and our judicial system, but the focus of the play centers around one juror, played by Henry Fonda, who is at first the sole holdout in an 11-1 guilty vote.

What makes this film so intriguing is the noise, the behavioral variability that occurs around the room. And what makes this story even more interesting is that this one juror is not spending energy in trying to prove the other jurors wrong, but rather on

---

[24] *12 Angry Men*. Based on the 1954 teleplay by Reginald Rose. The film version was released in 1957 and directed by Sidney Lumet.

getting them to look at the situation from a different point of view in order to reduce their personal feelings, and their biases.

I won't give away the ending, but I will say that this one holdout is able to influence the overwhelming odds. But the reason I have taken the time to discuss 12 Angry Men is because it hits upon a specific type of noise, and that's **group polarization**. The basic premise is that when people converse with one another, they tend to reach a point that is more extreme than their original inclinations. So if your initial tendency is to believe that your point of view has merit, by the end of the group engagement, you believe your point is absolutely the solution.

By the way, for those who may be wondering why this film, especially those listeners of a younger age, was written from the point of view of men only. This was not malice or to intentionally disregard women in any way. You need to think of the historical timeframe. The teleplay and film were produced in 1954 and 1957 respectively. At the time, women did not serve on the jury. It wasn't until the Civil Rights Act of 1957 that gave women the right to serve on federal juries, but it wasn't until 1975 that the United States Supreme Court established a constitutional protection for the right of women to serve on juries. I cannot help but wonder if 12 Angry Men had an influence at the time. In either case, this story has been produced as a play numerous times and nowadays usually goes by 12 Angry People with a more mixed group of actors.

This may be a good time to explain an area of confusion. Group amplification versus groupthink: Are they the same thing? Both complement one another, but they are not identical. Let me explain using this story.

For definitional purposes, groupthink is the practice of thinking or making decisions as a group in a way that discourages creativity or individual responsibility. It's when a cluster of people reach a consensus without critical reasoning or evaluation of the consequences or alternatives.

Think of this bias as the 11 out of 12 jurors who immediately and with mutual agreement pass judgment to come to a consensus of a guilty verdict in *12 Angry Men* (see box for details). However, each of those jurors may also be creating their own individual noise. They may be in immediate agreement, but each of them have produced their own individual noise, their own behavioral variability, to the table. Each creating their own noise, each clouding one another's judgment, each driving their separate belief systems, that also leads to that group polarization.

I have mentioned it before, but it helps to reiterate: consider groupthink as the bias, an observable error in judgment all heading in the same direction, whereas group amplification and group polarization as the dial that can ramp up and down the noise from individual influences.

Let's talk about ways to curb the influences of this type of behavioral variability:

**Actionable Step #1:**

*Don't try to change someone's mind.* Do help them look from a different perspective. Get people to discuss why they came to their point of view. Are there other variables you can introduce to their decision-making process that help produce other choices? So when it comes to your money, our minds like to narrow down choices to as simple a selection process as possible. But usually, it is not an either or, or black and white, decision; it is more gray. A quick example could be you are throwing a birthday party and you are trying to determine whether or not you should buy a cake or cupcakes. However, have you thought about baking a cake or cupcakes? That's an option for consideration too!

**Actionable Step #2:**

*Embrace conflict in your financial planning and decision-making.* Our inherent feelings of loss aversion, our fear of losing money, also make us highly susceptible to the influences of group amplification. The pressures to take action with our money based on what we see or hear in social channels and the media are highly influential. And at the same time, we tend to avoid conflict versus embrace conflict. We try to dodge statements and information that go against the amplified noises. Just the word, conflict, is considered something to avoid, but swap out the use of the word conflict with the word change and you might find it will give you an entirely new perspective on your ability to listen to opposing views.

**Actionable Step #3:**

*Stay focused on the agenda.* We spent a great deal of the start of this chapter talking about how group amplification can get us sidetracked. This may be one of the biggest challenges we have with managing our money. Intent vs. action. We want to save and invest more, but somehow less relevant, messages, voices interfere and tinker with those priorities.

All financial planning pretty much falls into three categories: Needs, wants and the unexpected. And maybe the problem is how we prioritize those three buckets. You want to save and invest for a new home, but you are craving to buy a new furniture set for your living room. While your kids are young, you want to save more for college, but you end up getting them the most ridiculously expensive toys they wanted from Santa this year. You hem and haw to save a few dollars every month on your phone plan, but you'll unnecessarily buy the latest smartphone model just because all your friends and family have the latest. In many of these situations, there is a catalyst, some amplifier, that is impacting your ability to prioritize your financial decisions.

**Actionable Step #4:**

*Play devil's advocate.* Go ahead, ask yourself, what are the consequences of not reacting to influential voices and messaging that you are exposed to? Ask incisive questions, think of comparable scenarios that refute the convincing claims, pose hypothetical situations to clarify and expand the inputs into a decision, and are there alternative explanations or solutions to the resulting judgments.

Going all the way back to our teaser about "what's for dinner?" I recommend steer clear of loaded, open-ended questions that lead to less relevant factors and simply offer a closed-ended question limited to two or three choices to reduce the noise. So what will it be, Chinese or Italian?

## Chapter Fifteen: Life Is Short…But Don't Short-Change Your Lifestyle
### Key behavior: Lifestyle Sustaining Income

*Have you ever heard of the children's book, "If you give a mouse a cookie?" It is a delightful tale if you are unfamiliar with the story. You see it starts off just as the title states: If you give a mouse a cookie, it is going to want a glass of milk. When you give him the milk, he'll probably ask you for a straw. When he's finished, he'll ask you for a napkin…and I think you can visualize that the reader is taken further and further down a spiraling story that continues with a mirror, scissors, broom, bed, crayons, picture drawing— leading up to scotch tape to hang that picture on a refrigerator, which brings the story full circle when the mouse becomes thirsty once again and will want a glass of milk. And if the mouse wants a glass of milk, it will want a cookie to go with that glass of milk.*

In this chapter, we're going to discuss how this illustrative picture book[25] published back in 1985 is strangely connected to the way we construct our own lifestyles.

So let's start with an innocent enough question: Have you ever formulated a list of New Year's resolutions or ever created such a list in the past? I think creating resolutions is very admirable. It shows that you seek self-improvement and growth and purpose and a desire for achievement in your life. According to various studies, there are always a few of the following that top the list for most people; and they are:

- Get into shape
- Eat healthier
- Lose weight
- Getting organized
- Quitting a vice such as alcohol, drugs or smoking
- Maybe it is a commitment to education or a new home
- Improve productivity and self-awareness
- Living more sustainable
- And of course, the one near and dear to my heart, bettering finances.

---

[25] Numeroff, Laura. If you give a mouse a cookie. Illustrated by Felicia Bond. HarperCollins Publishers. 1985.

But here's the thing, many studies[26] show by month 6, two-thirds of the American people abandon their resolutions. I would argue the reason for this is although these may all be worthy pursuits and create purpose-driven goals, it is behavior(the commitment) that drives those resolutions. In many cases, we are asking ourselves to change or adapt behavior. However, even if you want to change, it's really hard to do. If you are someone who has personally attempted to stick to your New Year's resolutions, you know how hard this really is. Changing behavior is about our emotions.

There's also another prevalent point to make. Notice the one common theme, one overarching connector to the resolutions we make annually and that's changes to our lifestyle. Regardless of the endeavor, if it relates to changing lifestyle, it often impacts your money management and the financial decisions you make in life. And the behaviors associated with those life events and alterations must be aligned with your behavioral-style and your financial wellness. The question to ask yourself is, "what **Lifestyle-Sustaining Income** do I require to satisfy the needs and wants I envision?"

So why is thinking in terms of a lifestyle sustaining income such a big deal. Well first off, I think we ignore it.

---

[26] https://discoverhappyhabits.com/new-years-resolution-statistics/ as an example supports this statistic.

You can hear it in our inner thoughts and socializations. When it comes to your desires, we often speak in terms of: I need this AND I want that AND I want do this AND I want to own that—as though we all have limitless financial resources, but we don't. And if you succumb to this line of thinking, it makes it extremely hard to achieve any one goal. More often than not, we should consider replacing the conjunction AND with the word OR (such as I need this or I want that). Like a twist on an old saying, you can pursue anything you want in life, but you cannot pursue everything...without repercussions.

### A PAYCHECK AWAY FROM BEING BROKE

I remember a time earlier in my career, living in a beautiful community north of New York City and I was one of those working on Wall Street as they say. And every early morning I would get to the train platform and stand with others who were commuting to the Big Apple. All of us followed our own professional pursuits as I was.

After a while, I became very friendly with this fellow commuter. His name was Jack. You could tell that he was further along in his career than I was and so was the respective paycheck. But here's the interesting thing, over time and comparing life notes I began to realize that there was quite the wealth gap. I was making $100,000 a year and Jack was making $1 million a year. Yet we were both a paycheck away from going broke. We both were failing at establishing a lifestyle-sustaining income.

> The point of this story is it doesn't matter how much you make, it is your ability to establish an affordable and attainable plan to achieve your goals.

There is the growing wealth gap that impacts all walks of life. We tend to assume that if you make a great deal of money, you have established an ideal financial situation. However, making more money does not necessarily equate to financial well-being. That's because there is an interdependency between money and your physical, mental and nutritional wellness too. But that is a whole other topic for a future discussion.

For now, think about money in its simplest form. It has only two tactical functions. One to buy stuff, and two to make more money with it. That's it. You have these two levers at your disposal to manage your money. It's also why having a budget or a financial plan is so important. They help to satisfy your needs, wants and the unexpected. But at the end of the day, your behavioral-style is tethered to and what defines your lifestyle.

Over the course of 14 chapters, we have discussed biases and behavioral variability that influence your judgements and money management. However, it's equally critical to establish what is an acceptable lifestyle and that lifestyle is highly susceptible to your emotions. Because folks, emotions are the building blocks of your personal preferences in life. Your goals are often aligned to them and so are your other life energies.

Which brings me back to the idea of New Year's resolutions. There's something else interesting about the most common resolutions that were listed earlier, they are often interconnected. One in particular, I'd like to hone in on and that's *getting organized*. I think that ought to be a prerequisite before tackling anything else. Just like any goal you establish, you need a plan and you need to get organized to create a plan.

Are you familiar with the Japanese art of decluttering and organizing? I'm talking about the craze that was started by Marie Kondo in the year's just before the pandemic. I believe over 10 million copies of her book[27] have sold to date and I even picked up a copy because who couldn't use a little more Feng shui in their home or at the office? I have to admit, I was quite skeptical and some of the learning lessons are self-evident, but just like anything we wish to improve upon, it sometimes helps to look through the problem with a different lens.

Many of the learning lessons that Kondo provides are applicable to addressing behavioral risks we face in decision making and an opportunity to improve one's lifestyle sustaining income. For

---

[27] Kondo, Marie. The Life-Changing Magic of Tidying Up: The Japanese Art of Decluttering and Organizing. Ten Speed Press. October 2014.

example, one of the first teachings is that people cannot change their habits without first changing their thinking.

These concepts behind tidying up, decluttering and organizing are not a final destination, but useful tools to keep you on course. Just as you re-examine your budget or financial plans on an ongoing basis and realign them. Maybe that's just it; we often review expenses, life events and the unexpected, but perhaps we don't give enough thought to changes in lifestyles.

This leads me to another book of relatable interest, *Essentialism*[28] by Greg McKeown. Possibly not as popular as *The life-changing magic of tidying up*, but nevertheless, another best seller that has sold millions of copies.

Why I gravitate to the concepts of essentialism is the advocacy to trim your life processes. Note I say processes versus stuff. That's because life is not just about stuff, it's about experiences too. Think about your desires beyond that new car, new home, new gadget, new garment. What about traveling, entertainment, hobbies, giving back to family or a cause?

So what's the connection to behavioral economics? Because just as biases and behavioral variability (or noise) are impacting your judgments, so too are they impacting your

---

[28] Mckeown, Greg. Essentialism: The Disciplined Pursuit of Less. Currency. April 2014.

chosen lifestyle, which in turn, influence your money management. Think about the title of this book: **Creating wealth starts with financial health**. In order to build wealth, you need to be aware of biases and filter through the noise.

If we tie this back to resolutions, we often create goals relating to what we want to stop doing, achieve greater materiality, or mastering a new skill. Ideally, a better mindset when choosing a path to achieve those goals is to hit the pause button and ask if you are investing your time and money in the most effective activities that are aligned to your behavioral-style and desired lifestyle.

Let's talk about several considerations you can take to establish your own lifestyle-sustaining income, after this brief message.

it's important to preface that while I found inspiration in the books mentioned, you may find your own inspiration through other sources. But as I also mentioned, sometimes it is just hearing similar advice through different perspectives. The reason I refer to both Kondo's and McKeown's books is the amazing synergy they have in terms of advice. Ironically, they both tie into financial wellness and address behavioral risks to managing money, whether it was even part of the author's intent.

I am going to reveal a few useful tips in a moment, but I realize that establishing a lifestyle sustaining income can be a comprehensive process inclusive of your EMOTIONAL needs and wants—as well as considerations of the unexpected—

should be incorporated into your financial planning. Whether you self-manage or work with a professional, I am sure there are those in the financial industry who may differ in approach. So please keep an open mind that my goal is not to give financial advice, rather tips on helping you understand and address behaviors that impact your judgments so you can potentially improve your chances of achieving your goals.

With that said, here are a few learning lessons associated with getting organized in order to reveal your own lifestyle sustaining income.

By the way, I have used that phrase probably a dozen or more times now: *lifestyle-sustaining income.* In essence, it emphasizes not living beyond your means and understanding the means necessary to support your emotional desires. Let's get to those tips:

**Actionable Step #1:**

*Remove the clutter.* It's an exercise to reexamine those needs and determine if they are truly essential. There's this famous German, industrial designer of consumer products named Dieter Rams.[29] He is known to embody the concept of less is better. [See box if you wish to dig deeper into this recommendation.]

---

[29] https://designmuseum.org/discover-design/all-stories/what-is-good-design-a-quick-look-at-dieter-rams-ten-principles

## LESS IS BETTER

Dieter Rams was all about the simple things in life by finding simplicity in everyday objects and activities. And if you wish to remove the clutter in your life, align with your behavior and design a lifestyle sustaining income, some of his principles may help. And they include:

a) Think out of the box and be innovative with your approach

b) Ask yourself the level of usefulness that a given need or want bring to your life

c) What is the aesthetic value? In other words, what is the human experience associated with your desires?

d) Does it support a level of fulfillment in your life that once achieved you will not need something more. Think about the *If You give a mouse a cookie* story we started with in this chapter.

e) Define the purpose AND the commitment needed to those things you want. That goes back to establishing viable resolutions.

f) Be honest with yourself. As mentioned earlier, you can pursue anything, but you cannot have everything.

g) Does it bring long-lasting joy? if you were to infuse a bit of Kondo's ideas, I would say don't just seek out what gives you feelings of joy today, rather what needs and wants in your life bring continuous joy. You will be surprised how many material goals become less of a priority.

h) If you want something, then it needs to be part of a plan. There needs to be a tentative path that leads to obtaining that need or want.

i) Is it something sustainable? This connects with some of the other points in terms of once you have it, can you keep it, does it continue to maintain a level of satisfaction in your life.

j) Don't make it complicated. I have a great analogy for this. Anyone a loyal Starbucks drinker? Despite having some very fancy espresso and cappuccino machines in my home, I still frequent Starbucks. And if you are a loyalty member you surely receive communications taunting and tempting you to purchase certain items for a limited time to get some Starbucks points added to your balance for free drinks, meals and other stuff. I'm a sucker for gamification too so throw on top of it something where you get game pieces or badges and I am all in. But how complicated did I make my life dedicating time and money to get a few points to get something "free"? That's not the best use of resources and nor is it when you choose to pursue needs and wants that are equally complicated.

## Actionable Step #2:

*It's hard to say no, so learn how to say yes.* In McKeown's and Kondo's and many other self-help books, advice is often given to mastering the ability to say no, to stay focused, to concentrate resources and avoid spreading yourself thin. It's sound advice, but if I may make a suggestion? It's hard to say no to things aligned with our desired lifestyle. Perhaps a slightly different lens would help. Rather than working up the willpower to say no, ask yourself what roadblocks, time and resources are required to say yes. It's not perfect, but this line of thinking will help you not only see the purpose of a need or want, but what kind of commitment and planning it will require if you choose to pursue it.

## Actionable Step #3:

*Avoid social pressures and the false beliefs of having it all.* I have read that the average person spends 2 and half hours a day on social media. It's become embedded in our regular routines in terms of communication, engagement and activities. It also influences our chosen lifestyles. At the same time, from a behavioral perspective, we often like to share what we have obtained and what we have achieved through social channels and not what was sacrificed to get there or in its place. There is research out there that states if you share your goals with others, you forge a greater commitment to those goals. I would just suggest not being so quick to share until you've followed the steps already mentioned so you are less likely to commit to needs and wants that really don't fit your lifestyle.

**Actionable Step #4:**

*Every need and want requires a routine.* If any goal, especially financially, is a hit and done...perhaps you have revealed an objective that is part of a bigger goal. Just like establishing resolutions...the commitment usually equates to a habit. Just like keeping a tidy home, establishing a lifestyle sustaining income takes routine efforts and a system to maintain.

**Actionable Step #5:**

*Don't forfeit your right to choose.* Once you start by saying I need this or I want that, you take away the power to influence your choices. Remember how I mentioned money is either good for buying stuff or making more money with it? It may be better to start with the assumption that what you desire is unessential until you can prove otherwise.

**Actionable Step #6:**

*Straddle your strategies.* Once you have established your life desires, your bucket list, can you find synergies amongst them. For example, going back once again to New Year's resolutions. If you had a desire to lose weight and exercise more, could you not think of routines and forging habits that both commitments complement one another? So, if we were to look toward financial wellness, are there activities you could take that are aligned toward meeting more than one purpose. For example, if you want to save more and have career growth, would pursuing additional education help more than one goal?

I'm going to stop here because I feel these basic actions may be enough of a nudge to help you rethink how your emotional desires influence your financial goals, and the required lifestyle sustaining income to fuel them.

But before we go, I want to get back to our children's story, if I may. The adventure of that little mouse is a circular message that builds on one want after another. You might even say it is a mousetrap or even a human trap, because how many of us create an overwhelming number of financially committed desires that force us to need ever more income to satiate.

Moral: Start with needs not wants, plan for the unexpected and only then should you decide if a cookie is what you really want. And if you do want that cookie … don't pick one that is so dry it requires a glass of milk.

# Conclusion

*I'll keep this brief because this is only the beginning, not the end, of your personal story.*

I hope you found this book to be educational, entertaining, and a source of inspiration. Most of all, I want you to feel empowered with the ability to recognize how your behavior can be a help or hindrance to your financial decision-making based on the lens you place on them. There are many more behaviors and emotions that can play havoc with our ability to manage our money. However, I have planted a few seeds in your brain so you can continue your exploration to financial wisdom.

To help you reflect on just how much you have learned, here is a recap of the concepts you now have a working knowledge of their influences:

- **Loss Aversion**: The fear of loss looms heavier in our minds than gains
- **Endowment Effect**: Overweighting the value of items and ideas we feel we own
- **Mental Accounting**: How we compartmentalize our money impacts our decisions

- **Delayed Gratification**: Patience has a positive effect on your financial future
- **Human Motivation Theory**: Control comes from power, achievement, or affiliation
- **Heuristics:** These are the short-cuts in your brain, often influenced by behavior, to make decisions
- **Framing Effect**: We react to only with the lens we see with
- **Experiential Bias**: Past learning lessons, don't always prove right in the future
- **Conformity Bias**: When a strong sense of belonging causes us to adapt to behaviors to fit into a group
- **Media Response Bias**: Media postings intentionally drive emotional reactions
- **Choice Paralysis**: An overwhelming number of choices can prevent a decision
- **Group Polarization**: The tendency for a group to make more extreme decisions
- **Anchoring Effect**: Limiting opportunity by comparing to a past experience
- **Confirmation Bias**: Seeking out info and advice that reinforces your beliefs
- **Behavioral Variability: Level Noise**[30]: Variability in an average judgment by different individuals

---

[30] Behavioral Variability descriptive labels from the book, Noise, written by Daniel Kahneman, Cass R. Sunstein, and Olivier Sibony.

- **Behavioral Variability: Pattern Noise**[30]: Variability in judgment from a single person
- **Behavioral Variability: Stable Pattern Noise**[30]: Variability in decisions based on personality differences despite similar contributing factors to a choice
- **Behavioral Variability: Occasion Noise**[30]: When your mood or your most recent experiences of a different decision impact your future choices
- **Behavioral Variability: Group Amplification**[30]: Personal, emotional feelings and beliefs are channeled through group decision-making
- **Lifestyle-Sustaining Income**: Anticipating your current and future needs and recognizing your ability to generate money versus outliving your wealth

Just look at how much knowledge you have gained. Feel good about the financial choices you make moving forward. Try not to reflect on past decisions that were less than optimal and become more optimistic about what you can do now.

*My only ask*: If you enjoyed this book, please share *FinWizdom* with your family, your friends, and anyone you know who could benefit from a deeper understanding of financial literacy.

Thank you for joining me on this journey and remember...

**Creating Wealth, Starts with Financial Health.**

## Free Bonus:

Podcasts are a great reinforcement tool as they promote active listening, which can potentially help you retain more of what you learned!

To continue your journey, visit www.finwizdom.com and subscribe to the *FinWizdom* podcast or find the program on your favorite podcast platform, and proceed to Season 4. If you are truly serious about retaining what you've learned, I encourage you to start from the beginning with Season 1.

## ABOUT THE AUTHOR

**Joel L. Franks** is the founder of FinWizdom and an adult financial literacy facilitator. He is an accomplished financial content developer, educator and trailblazer in applying behavioral finance to connect with an audience.

Joel is known for his keen ability to infuse behavioral economics when building content, messaging and deliverables that are relevant, engaging and shareable to a wide range of audiences. His career and influence spans across many notable financial firms, including several Fortune 500 companies. In addition, he has helped dozens of entrepreneurs and middle-sized organizations achieve desired growth and their goals—helping them sell more products, to more people, more often. He also teaches as an adjunct professor and presents at events large and small, but what is closest to Joel's heart is helping all walks of life attain financial well-being.

With extensive financial marketing experience in banking, investments and insurance, he offers a unique perspective to financial literacy. In addition to consulting for financial industry pioneers and giants, Joel is the host of the FinWizdom podcast series—an exploration of how your emotions influence your ability to manage money. He uses storytelling to explain investment concepts and various psychological biases that impact financial decision-making. His mission is to help individuals and organizations recognize behavioral risks and learn how to accommodate, not ignore, them.

Joel has several degrees and certificates obtained from Hofstra University, Pace University, New York University and Rutgers University. These range from a BBA and MBA in Marketing, a Certificate in Behavioral Finance and a Mini-MBA in Social Media Marketing.

He has residence in both New York City and in the vicinity of Charlotte, NC, and he takes advantage of what both have to offer in terms of culture, entertainment, foodie options, tennis and hiking adventures—often with his wife of more than 15 years. And when not out exploring, he is a voracious reader in a wide range of genres and continues to expand his knowledge around behavioral economics.